THE HEART of the HOMESTEAD

RUTHANN ZIMMERMAN

TEN PEAKS PRESS®
EUGENE, OR

Ephesians 6:4 is taken from the ESV® Bible (The Holy Bible, English Standard Version®), copyright © 2001 by Crossway, a publishing ministry of Good News Publishers. Used by permission. All rights reserved. The ESV text may not be quoted in any publication made available to the public by a Creative Commons license. The ESV may not be translated in whole or in part into any other language.

Matthew 6:19-21 is taken from the King James Version of the Bible.

Cover and interior design by Dugan Design Group
Photography by Jay Eads
Cover image (clouds) © two K / Adobe Stock

Illustrations © Zerbor / Shutterstock; © PyruosID / Adobe Stock; © Lifeking / Adobe Stock; © Arif Arisandi / Adobe Stock; © Alice July / Adobe Stock; © Vector Tradition / Adobe Stock; © THP Creative / Adobe Stock; © sense / Adobe Stock; © Muhammad / Adobe Stock; © Jen / Adobe Stock

For bulk or special sales, please call 1-800-547-8979.
Email: CustomerService@hhpbooks.com

 TEN PEAKS PRESS is a federally registered trademark of the Hawkins Children's LLC. Harvest House Publishers, Inc., is the exclusive licensee of this trademark.

Neither the author nor publisher is responsible for any outcome from use of this cookbook. The recipes are intended for informational purposes and those who have the appropriate culinary skills. USDA guidelines should always be followed in food preparation and canning. The author and publisher make no warranty, express or implied, in any recipe.

THE HEART OF THE HOMESTEAD

Copyright © 2025 by RuthAnn Zimmerman
Published by Ten Peaks Press, an imprint of Harvest House Publishers
Eugene, Oregon 97408

ISBN 978-0-7369-8976-3 (hardcover)
ISBN 978-0-7369-8977-0 (eBook)

Library of Congress Control Number: 2025931365

All rights reserved. No part of this publication may be reproduced, stored in a retrieval system, or transmitted in any form or by any means—electronic, mechanical, digital, photocopy, recording, or any other—except for brief quotations in printed reviews, without the prior permission of the publisher.

Printed in China

25 26 27 28 29 30 31 32 33 / RDS / 10 9 8 7 6 5 4 3 2 1

To my loving husband, Elvin, who believed I could.

To our children, who taught me to slow down and notice the heart.

CONTENTS

THE HEARTBEAT OF HOMESTEADING 7

1. GUIDED BY HOMESTEAD GOALS
   Working together as a family 13

2. FARM TO FAMILY TABLE
   Enjoying the feast and the fellowship 37

3. THE HOMESTEAD GARDEN
   Growing food for a growing family 67

4. FILLING THE LARDER
   Preserving the fruits of your labor 97

5. PIGS, POULTRY, AND PLANNING
   Embracing the learning curve 135

6. QUEEN OF THE HOMESTEAD
   Appreciating the family milk cow 165

7. THE ART OF THRIFTINESS
   Gaining contentment through a
   budget-friendly lifestyle 199

WHERE YOUR TREASURE LIES
   A few last and lasting words 217

RECIPE INDEX 221

THE HEARTBEAT OF HOMESTEADING

It is Friday night, our weekly family dinner night; the dining room walls are practically bulging with the activity they contain. Around the table, the family gathers as I take it all in from the kitchen. Elvin, my husband, at the head of the table, talks with a son-in-law about the engine in one of the trucks; our three daughters discuss a recent wedding in the family and the pending birth of the first grandchild; my ears pick up a couple statistics of a favorite sport and the verbal sparring of the younger children, who are elbowing each other for a position at the table and in the conversation.

The aroma of browned butter and homegrown beef permeates the air. As I place the final dish onto the laden table, I wipe my hands with a corner of my apron before removing it and hanging it on the hook. I seat myself at the table next to Elvin, place my hand in his, and expectantly wait for the familiar hush that will happen when the family takes notice that the meal is ready, the cook is seated, and we are ready to pray the prayer of thanks.

I take a deep breath and hold it for a second as if by inhaling and holding I can somehow keep this moment with me for eternity. This is it, I think; we are doing it! The years of toil and tears are paying off, and we are beginning to see the rewards for our efforts. Thoughts of thankfulness are now forever intertwined in my memory with the flavors of the meal and the comfort of conversation with family. I whisper a silent prayer of praise to the Father who walked with us every step of the way, for the days his love and faithfulness carried us. For the times he whispered encouragement to keep swimming against the current when all we wanted was to drift effortlessly downstream with the masses and rest our weary bodies and minds. For the wisdom he supplied at just the right time, and most of all, for the endurance he supplied to get us to this point of gratitude and joy in the journey.

Our reason for this way of life is not about the homegrown beef in the cast-iron dish. It is not about the homemade noodles or the garden-fresh peas and potatoes. It is not about the raw milk pudding we will have for dessert. It is about the family! The eternal souls that, at this moment, rest their feet under our table. Contrary to what many may think, we did not set out to grow the majority of our own food, and homesteading simply wasn't in our plans or even our vocabulary for many years. We simply set out to raise our family to have a hardy work ethic, a large dose of ingenuity, and the resourcefulness and skills needed to be a blessing to the world around them. We set out to raise children who will worship the Creator, have a heart for the unloved, and develop the emotional stability to be part of the solution. We set out to foster a family culture of togetherness, generosity, and servanthood.

We simply set out to raise our family to have a hardy work ethic, a large dose of ingenuity, and the resourcefulness and skills needed to be a blessing to the world around them.

OUR STARTING LINE

In numerous conversations, Elvin and I identified what we felt was significant in developing our character during our childhoods in the Old Order Mennonite families we grew up in: chores. There were cows to milk, eggs to gather, and dishes to wash—all before we rode our bikes to the one-room school each day. After school there were stalls to muck and more animals to feed, and there was laundry to do.

So, this is where we put our stake as the starting line for our family. Our children needed chores! The sole reason we ordered our first baby chicks was so our preschool-age daughters could learn to care for the needs of creatures other than themselves. I clearly remember those chickens becoming quite large before we finally harvested them, because the goal was not chicken in the freezer, the goal was the development of character in our children through responsibility.

As our family grew, the garden grew larger to accommodate their skills, and we added more animals to keep more children busy. We found ourselves purchasing more canning jars, another freezer, and additional fencing. Our family began to thrive in every way imaginable—not because everything went perfectly but simply because we were working together. Long hours spent in God's creation working in the soil, joyfully watching baby animals being born, and crying together over the losses of favorite animals or crops. As we watched our family thrive, we became inspired to look back to the old-fashioned culture of the first twenty-seven years of our lives for more insight into the slower-paced lifestyle that was conducive to reaching the family goals we were fully committed to achieving.

A few years ago, a friend and I were sitting in our backyard, snacking on homemade bread from my kitchen topped with butter made from our cows' raw milk and fresh jam made with strawberries from our garden.

"You are a true homesteader," she told me.

Confused, I asked for clarification, since, as far as I knew, the word *homesteader* was used in reference to those early American settlers who received land through working to improve it. Amused, my friend encouraged me to look up the hashtag #homesteading on social media, and that is when I discovered that there were hundreds and thousands of families seeking and actively working to recover the lost skills of their ancestors.

In the pages that follow, I hope that by sharing a bit of our journey I will not add more noise to a world that's already clamoring for your time, attention, and resources; rather, that through stories, simple recipes, our trials and errors, and Grandma's timeless wisdom, I will bring a quiet focus that helps you hear the very heartbeat behind the homesteading lifestyle.

CHAPTER ONE

GUIDED BY HOMESTEAD GOALS
Working together as a family

The climb from my childhood house down to the Conestoga creek was a treacherous one for an eight-year-old girl with a fishline in hand. My brother, older than me by two years, led the way with a fishline in one hand and tackle box in the other. We trekked a well-worn trail, and I knew every branch and rock foothold that we needed to get safely up and down the bank. The stretch of the Conestoga River that bordered our property was by no means a dangerous river; our carefulness while going up and down the bank was to avoid making a crash landing into the water like we did on swimming days.

We did not want to scare the fish away! After reaching the fishing hole, it was time to start flipping over rocks to find some bait for our lines. We were looking for earthworms, beetles, or the tails that the salamanders left behind in their rush to escape us.

On this day, my brother and I had the goal of catching a couple fish before Mom's whistle called us to take care of more chores. There were sure to be weeds to pull in the strawberry patch, horse stalls to muck, or potatoes to peel for dinner. However, for that moment we were free to follow our own interests, indulge our curiosity, and amuse ourselves. The knowledge that our free play was limited helped

The homestead life gave us a balance of both playing together and doing chores together.

us to cherish this time and use it wisely.

While as a child I couldn't have pinpointed the reason why I thrived, I now see how the homestead life gave us a balance of both playing together and doing chores together. We shared in co-creating our homestead experience. My enjoyable childhood has helped me to remain steadfast in providing opportunities for my kids to have similar times of exploration and unstructured play as well as the many lessons and benefits of chores.

I will admit that it hasn't always been easy. In the early years of managing chores with my own children, I often became frustrated with their bickering and whining when I made requests or when they ran out of steam before the assigned task was completed. I started to believe the lie that I wasn't a good mom and might as well give up. I lashed out at the children's less-than-willing attitudes instead of leaning into the Word of God and trying to understand the truth of raising children of principle.

Ephesians 6:4 teaches, "Do not provoke your children to anger, but bring them up in the discipline and instruction of the Lord." When I began the practice of viewing our daily homestead goals and chores as the daily opportunity to cultivate a righteous life, not only in myself but in our children as well, God gave me a much larger, future-reaching vision. No longer was an afternoon about weeding the garden; it was an opportunity for all of us to cultivate our character. It was an opportunity for me to trust that although there were complaints or grumblings, I wasn't failing as a parent. Even when the children entered the garden in ashes and sackcloth as they mourned the hour of play they had lost, I was being invited to work on my strength of spirit and character as I regulated my emotions and responded to them in a way that reflected the truth that we were working on a much larger goal than just weeding the garden.

A HEALTHY FAMILY SETS GOALS

Over the years, I have come to realize that when people express overwhelm or bafflement at the thought of a family our size, a primary

> A simple family goal kept in the forefront of your mind, for each life category, will be like a single beacon of light.

reason is because they're envisioning their own grocery bills, gym memberships, and wardrobe costs multiplied by the number of children they see around my shopping cart. They are imagining the occasional chaos of mealtimes and bedtimes and the battles of wills faced when it is homework time. Because they cannot fit the size of our family into the only lifestyle, budget, routines, and goals they are familiar with, they conclude that it can't be done—or it can't possibly be done joyfully, successfully, and with healthy results for all.

But the truth is, there are meaningful, doable ways through all seasons of parenting. Whether you have one child or ten, you can grow a homestead family of healthy, whole children—and adults, let's not forget ourselves—by setting long-term goals that guide your choices and echo your principles and priorities.

First, we set the goals. While you may have other categories, the core ones we focus on are:

- *Strength of spirit*
- *Strength of body*
- *Strength of mind*
- *Strength of character*
- *Strength of family*

The most effective long-term goals are simple. When we, as parents, are holding up every decision against the goal, we want it to be straightforward so no matter the ages of our children or the stage of family life we're in, we know when a choice or priority measures up.

The best goals allow for different personalities, interests, and gifts to flourish and for God to work individually in the life of each child, giving plenty of room for each member of the family to make mistakes, recognize those mistakes and misjudgments, and correct their actions.

A simple family goal kept in the forefront of your mind, for each life category, will be like a single beacon of light, helping you make

confident decisions as you go about your day. For example, if our goal is for our children to flourish in faith and be spiritually strong, then we teach them to pray and have a love for God's Word, and we make sure to set an example of spiritual priorities, such as family devotions, church, and youth group activities.

If our goal is strength of body, then we focus on providing the kind of nutritional support and opportunities for exercise that help us stay out of the doctor's office as much as possible.

If our goal is for our children to have an insatiable curiosity that spurs a lifelong joy of discovery and learning, then we make sure to protect their free play and create an environment of training, learning, and encouragement.

If our goal is to instill character, then we must fashion our days in a way that leaves time to work together on correcting mistakes and makes room for do-overs rather than simply rushing through to check things off a list.

If our goal is to foster strong family connections and relationships, then we may limit what children are involved in beyond the home so there aren't too many missed opportunities to work, dine, and play together as a family.

We adjust our lifestyle to fit our long-term goals.

FOLLOWING THE LIGHT OF YOUR GOALS

Take time to consider and name your goals. Discuss, shape, and clarify each one so you can return to them again and again. Then think about how to work toward them in practical ways. Following are some examples from my family that I hope will encourage you as you take simple steps to move toward your goals.

Strength of Spirit

Are my daily habits and attitude drawing the hearts of my family toward God for strength, help, and courage? Am I first teaching them how to pray before I offer a solution to a problem? Am I showing by example how to regulate my emotions in a frustrating situation?

As the beam of light that is your family's goal illuminates your days, you will find at the center a bright spot from which all other light reflects; without this bright spot, you simply have no light at all. This bright spot is the peace, will, and presence of God, and it will bring warmth and comfort to all who bask in it. The more time we, as parents, spend here, the more our family, drawn to us by relationship, is drawn to God's peace and wisdom.

Strength of Body

When I am shopping or cooking meals for the family, I hold the meals and shopping list up against the goal of strength of body. Is the nourishment and immune system support my family will receive from this food worth the price I am paying for it? Does the item and the price adequately justify the time it took to earn that amount of money? And finally, does this product and its ingredients support our long-term goal of healthy bodies?

My answers to these questions often inspire me to find a way to make a more nutritious version of a food, using my time instead of spending my money so that I can fill our pantry not only with select, healthy grocery store choices but also offerings from the homestead harvest.

If our goal is to foster strong family connections and relationships, then we may limit what children are involved in beyond the home.

Strength of Mind

The discipline of one's mind is a lifelong work that begins very early in life. Helping a child develop this strength looks a lot like asking them to give just a bit more when they decide they've had enough of a job. For example, assign jobs that you know are larger than the child's endurance or attention span; in this way you first give them the opportunity to stretch themselves to their own limit, and then, when they ask to quit, you can cheerfully say, "You've done a great job. If you mow to this edge of the house then you can quit."

When a child receives consistent praise, not only for a job well done but also for their self-discipline, they begin to learn to discipline their own mind.

Strength of Character

In our home, we view this practice as the ability to make God-honoring choices regardless of the influences around us. A person of strong character shows compassion, respect, and self-discipline in the face of adversity. The development of character in children flourishes with two components: the unconditional love and acceptance of their families and the examples of adults in their lives. And although it will develop slowly over a lifetime, the standards of character are set in those early years.

Strength of Family

Relationships are an important cornerstone of life, and every future relationship a child has will be built upon the experience of their first family relationships. Because relationships are best built upon shared experiences, it is important to incorporate as many as possible into our family life, such as dining together, working and playing together, and even settling differences.

The light of our long-term goal shining through behaviors paints a clear picture of what that behavior, if it becomes a habit, will look like in an adult. Seeing this allows me to help a child make small adjustments over time to get them lined up with our goal, while reminding myself not to expect perfection but to be happy with small improvements in line with each child's natural development.

As you journey toward your goals, stay encouraged and return to simple steps.

As you journey toward your goals, stay encouraged and return to simple steps. With growth, practice, and maturity, each member of the family will find their way closer to the center of the beam of light that is your goal.

CHILDHOOD CHORES AND YOUR FAMILY'S GOALS

Childhood chores were commonplace in the Mennonite culture of my childhood. There was the family cow to milk, there were dishes to wash, animals and humans to feed, and there was the weekly Saturday deep cleaning of the home. And although I alone didn't carry the burden of checking these chores off the list, I was responsible for doing what I was asked to do, when I was asked to do it. Most chores were done with a sibling or two to lighten the load and make the job more fun, and we had "big workdays" when the entire family would work toward a shared goal, such as harvesting chickens, preserving the harvest, or shelling peas.

A job well done will give them a dopamine reward that stimulates creativity, alertness, and focus.

Big workdays are at the core of many of my childhood memories. I do not remember the work as much as I do the camaraderie of the family. What felt like mundane and never-ending chores around the farm to ten-year-old me was really the feeling of developing the very character upon which my adult life is built!

When the mind is growing, the body has a need to be active. And when an activity has a purpose, a direction, and a goal, the developing brain forms strong connections that add up to lifelong skills and strengths.

Very young children are great at challenging themselves in both mental and physical ways with imaginary play. They learn to love the feeling of accomplishment they get from mastering small tasks. These small tasks turn into bigger ones, and eventually they feel they have mastered everything there is to conquer and are ready for more interesting challenges.

This next stage can be a frustrating one, as it suddenly requires more effort and forethought from parents. Children become bored with their current surroundings. They seem to lack creativity and imagination, and boredom sets in. Boredom is simply the search for a dopamine reward. Dopamine is one of the "feel good" hormones. This hormone helps us to stay alert, improves our focus, and boosts our creativity, just to name a few benefits. We all subconsciously chase that dopamine reward and naturally return to the place we last received this reward.

It is important to not respond to boredom with entertainment. Although entertainment gives a small dopamine reward, it often fails to challenge the mind or body and leaves us craving bigger and better entertainment. We must protect the developing brain from the artificial highs of video games and screen time. Every time a child satisfies their neurological need for a reward this way, they undermine the natural curiosity that directs their developing brains to find satisfaction in lifelong skills based on capability, leadership, and a strong work ethic.

Growth toward goals is a long, slow development requiring many hours of practice and patience.

As parents, it's not our job to fill every moment with activities or entertainment but rather to notice when a child needs a new challenge, something to conquer, and then to offer the opportunity through chores. The antidote for a child's boredom is a chore because a job well done will give them a dopamine reward that stimulates creativity, alertness, and focus. When a child learns to chase that dopamine high of a "job well done," they tend to rush through chores, taking shortcuts along the way, just to get to that high. This is a normal stage of development, and I, to this day, still find myself taking shortcuts occasionally because I am after that same dopamine reward! When the reward is gained not by rushing but through the satisfaction of contributing and successfully completing a challenging task, that becomes the goal they aim for.

Creativity and curiosity will displace boredom all day long! Childhood chores continue to stimulate the need to conquer and

master and give purpose and direction long after the child has outgrown the stage of imaginary play. For example, making the bed, peeling potatoes, and sweeping the floor are large accomplishments for a five-year-old child, but when they master these they will quickly become bored and subconsciously begin seeking another challenge.

After more than twenty years of parenting, I have learned that my kids' bickering and whining are the very sounds of their character developing. If my children don't have opportunities to complain about a chore, then I must consider that they might not have enough of or the right type of chores to grow and develop character.

◆ ◆ ◆

Once we recognize the significant role that childhood chores play in creating successful adults, we can shift our focus from a performance-based objective (checking jobs off a list) to one of developing lifelong character and skills. These lifelong skills take time and practice to put down deep roots that will serve a child well. We don't ever expect perfection, but we do expect growth. Growth toward goals is a long, slow development requiring many hours of practice and patience. The chores of the home and homestead are merely the tools used.

No matter which childhood chores are available to your family, implementing them into your children's routines helps them develop toward your long-term goals, and while working on those character skills through chores, they will be picking up a great set of life skills.

CHORES DON'T NEED TO BE A CHORE

It is not hard to convince most parents that chores can build character and support a family's goals. More difficult, however, is to convince them that their kids will actually do the chores. If you're a bit skeptical yourself or you've had problems before, I promise, there is a way. You just have to start, be consistent, and extend a lot of grace to yourself and your children. No matter if you're introducing chores to a child who is three or thirteen, the process is the same—start small and build on the skills mastered. When a child masters feeding a pet or homestead animal, then we add another chore to that. In this way, as the child grows in physical strength and the brain development takes place, the chores assigned keep them growing and challenged.

When a child is new to chores, my husband and I work closely beside them, allowing our own positive attitude about chores to set the tone. We're careful not to criticize and, instead, always encourage them to grow and master the skill. We avoid being legalistic about the way a chore is done and instead help the child understand the result of the chore in such a way that they can choose for themselves how to get the desired outcome.

We make this last part very simple and clear:

Here is the result we want . . .

Here is the way I do it.

And then we leave the child to develop their own method.

When we leave a child to develop their own system of doing a chore, we stay close enough to give redirection or reminders to prevent any bad habits from settling in but not so involved that the chore remains or becomes our responsibility.

The willing but not able stage: Toddler and preschool years. By bringing the toddler or preschooler alongside your work, praising them for efforts and helpfulness, you are sending the message that they are a necessary part of the home and homestead's daily operations. You will be able to build upon this foundation of belonging through the next two stages. This is a very important stage and should be valued for willingness rather than strength or skill.

The able but not willing stage: Elementary ages. You will know it when your child gets to this stage. Trying to make you believe that they lack ability, strength, and skill seems to be the goal for this age group. This age group gets quickly overwhelmed with lengthy chores, and it is important to work side by side with them on bigger jobs.

For example: Washing the family's dinner dishes looks overwhelming to an eleven-year-old. The child shifts their goal to getting

out of the chore by feigning incompetence because they don't yet have the experience or brain development to see the bigger goal of getting all the dishes done and getting that dopamine hit of a job well done. I help shift the goal by saying something like, "Let's get a good start and have a good attitude, and then when you get to the pots and pans we will reevaluate the job." In this way we are breaking the job up into smaller bites and giving the goal of a good attitude rather than just a job executed. And then I find work to do in close proximity, helping them a bit here and there to keep them encouraged with my good attitude and positive influence.

The willing and able stage: Also known as the teenage years. This is the golden age of childhood chores and in my experience passes in a flash. Teens have the skills to work like an adult and can make a big difference around the home and homestead. The biggest challenge for this age group is that they have their own ideas on how and when things could get done, and it is helpful to give them the space to set their own goals.

For example, rather than saying, "Come, we are going to clean the pigpen," like you would to a younger child, you will now say something like, "The pigpen really needs to be cleaned. Can you please do it sometime before Saturday?" In this way you are giving them responsibility but allowing them the freedom to refine their time management and taking responsibility skills.

"Complaining is always heard but never rewarded" is a good motto for a parent to have through all stages. By hearing your children's complaints, you are understanding where they are in their development of character and skills and can adjust your expectations accordingly while at the same time encouraging them to grow in strength, skill, and character.

We aren't expecting perfectly executed chores because that serves us well. We are expecting growth of character because that's what will serve the child well for the rest of his or her life.

> We are expecting growth of character because that's what will serve the child well for the rest of his or her life.

KEEP YOUR EYE ON THE PRIZE

Let's go back to my example of the kids grumbling about having to weed the garden. That time is about so much more than the wellness of a piece of our property. It is an opportunity for my children to develop strength of character, body, spirit, and mind. As we work together in the soil and among the plants, the number one question is, of course, "When will this be over?" I engage them to develop their strength of mind by asking them to keep at it just a bit longer than they think they have the ability or desire to handle. By doing this, I am also encouraging them to stretch and grow their physical endurance—their strength of body. I invite them to build up their character and spirit by requiring a good attitude and asking them to be faithful in honoring my parental authority, their integrity, and the stewardship of God's creation.

We work on the strength of family through shared experiences and shared goals because working together, even when there are less than stellar attitudes, is still a family experience that strengthens relationships.

The homestead life presents many times when a do-it-yourself mindset is the best one. But when it comes to a homestead chore, doing it myself every time will not bear the fruit of a healthy family. I remind myself daily that although doing chores by myself reaches my short-term goals of peace and having things done my way, it is much better to work on our long-term goals by allowing the children to help shoulder the responsibilities and reap the rewards.

After all, life skills aren't created with one job done well; they are created by stringing a whole list of childhood chores (and mistakes) together with time management, responsibility, and work ethic to form a beautiful gift that your child won't fully comprehend until adulthood. Through it all—the challenges and the teaching—our end goal is not for our children to grow up and honor us for their childhood but to become successful and competent adults who bring glory and honor to their heavenly Father.

HOMESTEAD CHORES FOR EVERY AGE

Ages 2 to 4 (supervised):

- [ ] Help sort laundry
- [ ] Help fold laundry
- [ ] Put clean clothes in proper drawers
- [ ] Set the table for a meal
- [ ] Rinse dishes when someone is washing
- [ ] Help put clean dishes away
- [ ] Help make beds
- [ ] Help pick up toys
- [ ] Help carry supplies for any chore parents are doing
- [ ] Hold clothespins and hand them to the person hanging laundry to dry
- [ ] Scoop animal feed into buckets
- [ ] Bring veggies from the cold room
- [ ] Feed small animals
- [ ] Gather eggs

Ages 5 to 9 (mastered the 2 to 4 list and working on the following):

- [ ] Sort laundry
- [ ] Know how to run washer and dryer
- [ ] Hang laundry on the line
- [ ] Fold and put laundry in proper places
- [ ] Make bed
- [ ] Wash dishes
- [ ] Stack dishes into dishwasher
- [ ] Dry and put away dishes
- [ ] Set table properly
- [ ] Make scrambled eggs
- [ ] Make toast and other simple side dishes
- [ ] Pack own lunch
- [ ] Gather, wash, and store eggs
- [ ] Feed animals

Ages 5 to 9 (continued):

- [ ] Help milk cows or goats
- [ ] Open and close farm gates
- [ ] Pull weeds
- [ ] Help put down compost
- [ ] Help harvest from the garden and orchard
- [ ] Help with cleaning veggies for canning
- [ ] Bring jars of food from the cold room
- [ ] Take empty jars to storage
- [ ] Help clean animal stalls
- [ ] Take out garbage

Ages 10 to 16 (mastered the 5 to 9 list and working on the following):

- [ ] Do laundry independently from start to finish
- [ ] Keep bedroom clean
- [ ] Prepare and serve simple meals
- [ ] Set a family-style table for guests
- [ ] Clean kitchen after cooking
- [ ] Watch younger siblings without an adult's presence
- [ ] Keep a home clean while watching younger siblings
- [ ] Do animal chores independently
- [ ] Milk cows or goats independently
- [ ] Muck out animal stalls and take care of compost
- [ ] Operate small equipment and power tools safely
- [ ] Recognize weeds and work independently in the garden
- [ ] Distinguish between ripe and unripe fruit and veggies well enough to harvest independently
- [ ] Know the basics of canning and preserving; able to proceed with simple steps on their own
- [ ] Burn trash safely
- [ ] Take over adult chores for a short period of time

CHAPTER TWO

FARM TO FAMILY TABLE
Enjoying the feast and the fellowship

The family table is at the very core of most of my childhood memories. My dad sat at the head, my mom to his right, and a baby or toddler in the high chair between them. We had assigned seats at mealtime, the younger ones being closest to Mom and Dad while my older siblings were seated farther away. Meals were always served family style. When everyone was seated, we would have a silent prayer of thanksgiving, and then dishes of food were passed in an orderly fashion around the table until everyone was served.

These mealtimes, especially the more relaxed evening meals, involved much laughter and storytelling, solving problems, and discussing community news. My older siblings shared about their first jobs and first dating experiences. The younger children shared about their day and what they were learning or how they helped around the homestead that day. It was a time of connection.

My grandma, even when it was only her and Grandpa, would set a formal table for every meal she made, then walk out onto her porch and ring the dinner bell. Grandpa would come promptly, wash his hands and face, and sit at the table with a smile. He would ask the blessing and thank Grandma for the effort. After the meal he would thank her again, this

As a child, all I knew was that the shared time around our evening meal (or any meal) made me feel loved and safe.

time for the delicious food. This was their habit. It was a habit of togetherness, of generosity, and of servanthood. The impact of seeing such kindness and partnership modeled was significant.

As a child, all I knew was that the shared time around our evening meal (or any meal) made me feel loved and safe. I experienced a deep sense of belonging. Now I realize that this was where a large portion of our family culture was developed.

Family culture influences the way we think, feel, and act on a daily basis. It helps us develop morals, values, and problem-solving skills. From big life decisions to small choices, our family culture plays a large role in our adult life.

Not only did my mom bring nourishing food to the table for the family, but she and Dad partnered to create an atmosphere that nourished our souls and encouraged a healthy family culture.

I hope this journey inspires you to nourish your family both inside and out.

SIMPLIFY INGREDIENTS AND INCREASE NUTRIENTS

Cooking from scratch allows you to simplify your ingredients and add more nutritional value to your meals. It gives you control to prepare food that nourishes bodies rather than merely fills bellies.

Fast food and convenience foods are those created by large corporations with the goal of profit. They use the cheapest ingredients and then develop a packaging and marketing plan to bring them the most profit possible. These convenience foods have long lists of cheap ingredients and an even longer shelf life and take little to no effort to prepare for serving.

Slow food is what it sounds like—the opposite of fast food. Slow food is prepared from a few simple ingredients that are grown and preserved in a way that keeps their nutrients intact and then served

Not only did my mom bring nourishing food to the table for the family, but she and Dad partnered to create an atmosphere that nourished our souls and encouraged a healthy family culture.

with the intention of nourishing the body. These foods often take time and effort to prepare for serving.

Simplifying the ingredients your family consumes can be done over time and with a bit of data collecting and research. Take note of the groceries you buy regularly for your family and decide which ones to simplify first by reading the ingredients list. Those with the longest list of ingredients are the first to get replaced because those are likely the foods with elements that you and I wouldn't identify as food and, in some cases, have ingredients that could be identified as toxins. Ask yourself the simple question, "Can I learn to make this at home?"

When you learn that a bread recipe can be as simple as flour, water, and salt, you will start questioning the twelve or more ingredients listed on the bag of the bread you buy weekly. As your skill of reading ingredients develops, you will likely become more appalled at the number of unnecessary ingredients your family is consuming. Sometimes cutting out ingredients is as simple as switching to a different brand, but I discovered that buying a purer version with a shorter list of ingredients is typically a much pricier option, causing me to still choose to make the item from scratch.

Cooking from scratch is a large undertaking and one that can seem overwhelming, especially if you are new to kitchen skills. Cooking from scratch is not an overnight transformation; if you try

Cooking from scratch is a large undertaking... especially if you are new to kitchen skills.

to transform overnight, you will get burdened down and discouraged! It takes time to develop new skills, and cooking is no different. It might take you a week or even a month to master each new recipe and skill, but don't become discouraged. If one recipe isn't working for you, try someone else's method or recipe until you find one that your family loves and that is simple for you to make. Not every new recipe and skill will take as much time and effort as the first couple do. And just because a recipe is one family's favorite doesn't mean that it will work for your family.

Each new skill you learn will build on a previous skill mastered, and each new recipe will become easier until you have a complete skill set to draw from and experiment with. When changes to your cooking skills are made slowly and with intention and time for skill mastery, they will add up to become a lifestyle change.

BUYING IN BULK

As your skill set grows, your grocery list will shrink. When you're noticing the same simple ingredient items on your list week after week, you are ready to purchase those items in bulk. These simple ingredients are all going to work together beautifully in different ways to create nourishing meals for your family.

Flour, sugar, oats, nuts, beans, rice, and salt are a few of the staples that we purchase in bulk and store in food-grade five-gallon buckets. These staples—along with the hundreds of jars of food we grow and preserve, the freezers full of meat we have grown, and dairy from our cows—are the foundation on which every one of our meals is built. (We do have the occasional birthday meal request that requires us to purchase special ingredients.)

When you begin the habit of buying ingredients in bulk, you'll want to start slowly. Let's take flour as an example. Flour is a simple ingredient in so many recipes, including those for many kinds of breads, buns, and rolls; gravy mixes and sauces like Alfredo and other cheese sauces; and specialty baked goods. When I buy one hundred pounds of flour, I want to be positive that it is a flour that really serves our needs. When I began buying in bulk, I started with an order of ten pounds each of a couple different brands of flour. I then was able to compare and decide which worked best for our needs.

Not all flours are created equal, even when they are labeled the same. I learned this when learning to bake with sourdough starter. The organic flour from a smaller company performed better in all my recipes than the cheaper all-purpose flour from the grocery store shelf. Purchasing from smaller companies will ensure that your flour is fresh. And storing it properly will keep it fresh. We now buy enough flour to last us almost half a year and store it in food-grade five-gallon buckets with Gamma Seal lids. We do the same with sugar and oats. Gamma Seal lids have a rubber gasket that, when turned tight, seals the lid, preventing any bugs from getting in.

Nuts, salt, rice, beans—these are ingredients we use in lesser quantities, so these get stored in two-gallon buckets. Other options are available for bulk food storage, and with a little research you will be able to find one that works for your space.

As your skills develop and your grocery list dwindles, your time in the kitchen increases. There will be many more dishes to wash and messes to clean up (unless you are a tidier cook than I am). I remind myself that nothing is free. I'm paying with time when I choose to cook from scratch. But I'm willing to pay with time if it means my time is buying better health and nutrition for the ones I love. And with practice, you, too, will become more efficient in the kitchen, cutting down on the time it takes to clean up.

SHORTENING YOUR SUPPLY CHAIN

Becoming conscious of your supply chain is important when you're a cook-from-scratch homemaker. The moment you shift to serving foods with ingredients that go from the farm to your family table or you seek the shortest distance from the original source to your home, you become aware of how unnecessary many of your past commercial purchases have been.

Your supply chain consists of all the folks who must show up for work to get supplies to your home, the ingredients needed to grow or create an item, and the modes of transportation to get anything you rely on from source to home.

Let's take something simple like canned green beans as an example. The seeds are planted by machine; chemically treated for weeds, pests, and diseases; and finally harvested by machine. Dozens of folks are involved in the process of growing green beans, and all of them are primarily motivated by a paycheck. After being harvested, the beans are trucked hundreds of miles to canneries—often in open trucks with the sun beating down on them—and at the canneries are hundreds more people who punched the clock that morning. The beans then have another journey of countless miles from the cannery to warehouses all over the country.

Becoming conscious of your supply chain is important when you're a cook-from-scratch homemaker.

At the warehouses are more folks working hard for those paychecks. The next trip the green beans take is from the warehouse to the grocery store shelves, where finally people in your local community work to unload the green beans and stack them onto the shelves where finally you find them. And there's only one more person who had to show up for work that day before you can take the green beans home to feed your family: the cashier. Everyone in between you and your dish of green beans showed up to collect a paycheck, and you'll never even know the folks behind the big companies that profited most from the crop they raised.

And what happens if those folks don't show up for work? People around the world found out during the pandemic. When factories, warehouses, restaurants, and even some stores were temporarily closed, everyone faced discovering where their food comes from. It was a wake-up call for many families, and even better, it was motivation to become a bit more self-sufficient, even if that was as simple as making bread or some other staple at home. This world event became an invitation to everyone to pay attention and start doing a few things or a lot of things differently.

Becoming aware of your supply chain is the first step to shortening it!

Let's keep looking at the green beans. There are a few simple options to drastically shorten your supply chain.

You can grow the green beans yourself. You can buy the seeds (after your first crop, you can save your own seeds and eliminate this step), plant and tend the seeds, gather your harvest, then clean and preserve the green beans. The only person involved in getting your green beans from your garden to your family table is you and maybe your kids if they helped with this chore. That's a mighty short supply chain, not to mention all the nutrients you preserve by preserving them at home, within hours after harvest.

You may not be able to garden and grow green beans yourself, but you can still shorten your supply chain dramatically by connecting with a local grower through a farmers market or CSA (Community

TIP: Connecting with smaller farms, growers, and producers is the number one way to shorten your supply chain for all the items you cannot grow and produce yourself.

Supported Agriculture) program. When you find such a program, you will be able to directly connect with the grower, who has likely been up since the break of dawn picking the green beans that you are going to buy and take home and preserve before they've even been off the stem for twenty-four hours. Now you have two people in your supply chain—the grower and yourself.

ADJUSTING THE FAMILY PALATE

When you start cooking from scratch and eliminating ingredients, your family will notice. And I also predict they will clearly let you know that they prefer the store-bought version over your homemade or homegrown version, thank you very much.

When our older two daughters started attending a private Christian school after being homeschooled, they became aware of the difference between their from-scratch lunches and the other children's lunches full of processed food options. They started asking for Lunchables, SpaghettiOs, ramen noodles, and microwaveable mac 'n' cheese. I'd respond with the simple answer, "That's too expensive." I knew I could pack their lunches for a fraction of the cost. Because I didn't fully explain the many reasons that we weren't buying those kinds of foods for their lunches, they assumed that we were poor and their classmates were rich. They started calling convenience food "rich people food" and still do to this day.

The goal is to educate our children and arm them with the information they need for the day when they are responsible for their own nutrition.

I'm now further along in my parenting journey and have learned to take a balanced approach of making sure to educate my children more thoroughly on why we don't buy these packaged foods, teaching them to read the labels along with me, and helping them understand how their bodies respond to additives like food dye and preservatives. Taking this balanced approach helps our children understand why these foods don't have a permanent spot in our pantry but rather are an occasional treat. I don't want to villainize these foods and take a legalistic approach to our family's diet. Rather, the goal is to educate our children and arm them with the information they need for the day when they are responsible for their own nutrition.

These boxed and bagged convenience foods contain many flavor enhancers and additives that are immensely pleasing to the taste buds and that spark our cravings for these foods. It's a slow process when we wean ourselves and our families from these convenience foods that add so many unnecessary and unhealthy ingredients to our diets.

Let's take chips as an example. Chips are extremely expensive, have little to no nutritional value, and even have many additives and ingredients that are detrimental to my family's health. My family was in the habit of having chips in their lunch every day, and of course their favorites were the brands and flavors that were most expensive and had the longest list of ingredients.

As we slowly eliminated one processed food after another from our diet, chips were one of the last to go. Because the question "Could I make these at home?" wasn't easily answered, these pricey favorites stayed on our grocery list month after month.

After much thought, I decided on popcorn as a solution. I pop it in natural animal fat—we use tallow or lard, which makes it quite tasty. This snack of three ingredients—corn, oil (fat), and salt—is very satisfying and far healthier than purchased snacks and chips that have thirty ingredients. I also sometimes make a special caramel popcorn version that everyone loves and considers a more-than-adequate substitution for chips.

I made the change over time, because had I removed all the favorite snacks at once, I would've faced a revolt. And I probably would've thrown in the towel and decided that it wasn't worth the strife. So, I cut back on the chips I bought and filled in the non-chip days with popcorn. This also gave me time to adjust to the extra work that making popcorn caused.

The children adapted and learned to fill their lunches with healthier options like cheese, meat, and fruit that we kept on hand.

We now purchase chips as a treat for special occasions, but they are no longer a part of our everyday diet. I also started making homemade granola bars as a wholesome, limited-ingredient snack.

It takes time for the family's palate to adjust. Sometimes it's a texture issue and they are slow to warm up to a new homemade food because they miss the stabilizers that corporations use to keep the texture integrity of their foods. My family has been extremely slow to warm up to homemade bread. I have tried many different recipes and methods, and after years of trying I still have family members who don't like to use homemade bread for their sandwiches even if they will eat the homemade version as toast with a bit of butter and honey.

I've tried the approach of not buying any bread and only having homemade bread available to them, but alas, they just stopped eating sandwiches. I continue to bake bread, as the majority of the family has accepted homemade bread as the new normal for our pantry. The grumbling has slowed down considerably, and the younger children don't seem to have a preference for store-bought bread anymore.

In general, the younger a child is when we replace their foods with homemade or healthier options, the faster their palate adjusts to the new taste and texture of homemade foods and the sooner they forget what the store-bought versions tasted like. There are many

I continue to bake bread, as the majority of the family has accepted homemade bread as the new normal for our pantry.

foods that I wish I had replaced sooner in our family, but during certain seasons I couldn't imagine adding one more job to my list of responsibilities.

And sometimes I have to commit to stop buying something in order to motivate myself to learn to make something from scratch, as was the case with tortillas. After a couple months of no tortillas, I and my family got so hungry for them that I was forced to learn how to make them!

FAMILY STYLE DINING

Now that you are spending more time in the kitchen and are putting so much effort into cooking from scratch, it seems only right that your meals should be served with a little intention. Family-style dining will not only be a beautiful way to showcase the meals you're cooking, it will bring you closer as a family.

The level of formality at your table is completely up to what works for your family.

The level of formality at your table is completely up to what works for your family. And if it has been a while since you've had the whole family together for a shared meal, just keep your end goal in mind and stay committed to small steps and decisions that will eventually shift your household toward new, healthy habits.

My formal style for a meal is far from fancy. I set the table with nondisposable plates, cups, napkins, and utensils and use a tablecloth. The tablecloth adds another level of formality and helps catch the crumbs and mess that we then shake out the door for the cats and dogs after each meal. The effort and the result do not have to be difficult or perfect for it to feel purposeful and lovely.

When the table has been set (this is a great chore for preschool and early elementary age children) and the meal prepared, we set all the dishes of food, plus pickles or other sides, onto the table and the family gathers. We hold hands and ask a blessing on the food, which we then pass around the table, and everyone gets served. Smaller children sit next to adults or older siblings who can help them with the large dishes of food and other needs they might have during the meal.

We practice table manners from the time the children are toddlers and continue to work on them at every meal. The family table is where we catch up on each other's day and share about things we experienced. It's a great place for us to praise the children for things they have accomplished or mastered or are working on. We often have deep discussions about events happening in the world or community. But most important of all, it's the place where Elvin and I together have the chance to shepherd and lead our children's hearts to deeper faith in and dependence on God through devotions and prayer, and by example of how we respond to different conversations and events happening near and far.

God created children with an automated maturation mechanism that helps them grow and learn. When they are newborns, they mimic the facial expressions and copy behaviors of those they are bonding with. We can easily forget that this mimic-and-copy instinct stays active well into adulthood. The family meal table is a great place for children to engage with and learn from the adults in their lives. Even if your child seems focused on their plate of lasagna and not on you, they notice how each person treats the others.

◆ ◆ ◆

As community events and world events are discussed at the family table, you, as a parent, get to greatly influence the way your family reacts to these events and how these events shape the lives of your children. When you understand how loud the world and its influence really are in the lives of your children, especially teenagers and young adults, you'll desire to commit to family mealtimes as many days of the week as you can to create a secure family culture for your children to grow up in.

If you only have the capacity to make a few minor changes in your family's routine, I would absolutely recommend spending every possible mealtime together as a family gathered around the table.

Even when all the family is not home, even when I am using disposable plates and flatware, and even if I am serving boxed convenience meals, the family meal table is a place of joy and connection. A fast-food meal served at the family table and enjoyed with laughter and conversation is still better than a top quality, made-from-scratch meal served with bitterness and consumed while each member of the family is in a separate world lived out on a tiny screen.

The souls that sit around your dining room table are eternal souls and are well worth the time and effort of planning how and what you serve. Preparing a family table welcomes everyone to be a part of the conversation, the love, the fellowship.

I would absolutely recommend spending every possible mealtime together as a family gathered around the table.

WHITE BREAD
Makes 2 loaves

DIRECTIONS

In a large mixing bowl, mix 1 cup water with the yeast and honey. Let it sit until foam appears on the surface, about 5 to 10 minutes. Add the remaining water with the salt and oil.

Add 2 to 3 cups of flour and mix to form a smooth dough. Continue to add flour, ½ cup to a cup at a time, until you get to 5 cups.

Knead for 5 to 10 minutes. Let the dough rest for 10 minutes and then knead for another 5 minutes. If at this point the dough is still sticky, add about ¼ cup of flour and then start the kneading and resting steps again. Continue to add flour and knead until you have a dough that is smooth, elastic, and no longer sticky. Cover the dough with a lint-free towel, then set in a warm place to allow the dough to rise.

Once it has doubled in size, divide the dough into two even pieces and shape into loaves. Place your loaves into greased loaf pans, cover, and let rise until it doesn't spring back when you poke it with your finger.

Bake in a preheated oven at 375° for 25 to 35 minutes or until the internal temp of the loaf has reached 190°.

Remove from the oven and brush the tops with butter.

INGREDIENTS

2½ cups warm water, divided

1 T. instant yeast

½ cup honey

2 T. salt

3 T. oil (I use melted tallow or butter)

5 to 7 cups all-purpose flour, divided

Butter

GRANOLA BARS
Yields 8 to 12 bars

DIRECTIONS

In a large bowl, mix Rice Krispies, oats, nuts, and dried fruit; set aside.

In a small saucepan over medium-low heat, melt the honey and nut butter, then add vanilla. Pour over the Rice Krispies mixture and mix thoroughly.

Press mixture into a 9 × 13-inch pan and chill, then cut into squares.

Use any combination of seeds, nuts, and fruit to your family's preference.

INGREDIENTS

3 cups Rice Krispies

2 cups rolled oats

½ cup finely chopped nuts or nut/seed combination

½ cup finely chopped dried fruit

1 cup honey

1 cup nut butter (we use natural peanut butter)

1 tsp. vanilla

CARAMEL POPCORN
Yields 1 gallon

DIRECTIONS

Pop popcorn and set aside. In medium saucepan over medium-low heat, melt butter, brown sugar, and maple syrup and then simmer for 5 minutes. Remove from heat, wait for simmering to stop, then add salt, vanilla, and baking soda. Mix thoroughly and pour over the popcorn. Stir gently to partially cover all popcorn.

Bake at 250° for 45 minutes, stirring every 15 minutes.

Cool to room temp and store in airtight containers.

Caramel popcorn is shelf stable for a month or more and can be frozen for 6 or more months.

INGREDIENTS

6 quarts popped corn, lightly salted

1 cup butter

2 cups packed brown sugar

½ cup pure maple syrup

1 tsp. salt

2 T. vanilla

½ tsp. baking soda

CREAM SOUP

Makes 10 to 12 oz. (equivalent of one can of soup)

DIRECTIONS

In a heavy-bottom pot, sauté your veggies, mushrooms, or chicken and optional onion and garlic in the fat to help them release their flavor.

Turn heat to medium-low and stir flour into the sautéed veggies or chicken until a smooth paste is formed.

Add broth or water, milk or cream, and salt and pepper.

Simmer until desired thickness is reached, making sure to stir often, scraping the bottom to keep mixture from scorching.

Use this in any recipe that calls for a cream soup. Keep in refrigerator for up to 2 weeks or freezer for up to 6 months.

INGREDIENTS

¼ to ½ cup finely chopped celery, mushrooms, or chicken

Optional: chopped onion, chopped garlic, to taste

3 T. fat (butter, lard, tallow, or bacon grease)

4 T. flour

½ cup chicken broth or water

½ cup milk or cream

¼ to ½ tsp. salt

¼ tsp. black pepper

GREEN BEAN CASSEROLE

Serves 12 to 15

DIRECTIONS

In a heavy-bottom pot, prepare one recipe of Cream Soup; mushroom or onion is our family's favorite. Gently stir in the green beans. Transfer into a 9 × 13-inch pan.

Melt the butter and mix with breadcrumbs. (I collect loaf end pieces or broken bread slices in the freezer and use for recipes that call for breadcrumbs.) Sprinkle breadcrumbs on top of the green bean mixture and bake at 350° for 30 minutes.

INGREDIENTS

1 recipe Cream Soup (above)

2 quarts green beans, drained

1 T. butter

½ cup breadcrumbs

◆ CHAPTER THREE ◆

THE HOMESTEAD GARDEN
Growing food for a growing family

I carefully used the tweezers and plucked the tiny crimson stigmas from the purple flowers, dropping the delicate harvest into the glass jar provided by my grandma. The area where the Crocus sativus grew was my favorite place in Grandma's garden. I took the responsibility so seriously that I checked multiple times a day to see if any more of the purple crocus flowers had opened, offering their harvest to me. These crimson stigmas are used all over the world as a delicate spice known as saffron. (It's important to distinguish these from the autumn crocus—Colchicum autumnale—which are poisonous.) Being entrusted with the harvest of this valuable spice made me feel much older than my ten years and oh, so important.

This tiny jar of saffron resided in Grandma's spice cupboard, and although I'm sure Grandma used the saffron in many places, the only memory I have of her using it is when she would drop a couple stigma threads into a pot of boiling water and then add her homemade noodles. This unique spice gave the homemade noodles a vibrant yellow color and a taste between earthy and floral.

My mom tells me that I was practically raised in the garden. Born in early April, I spent much of my first summer on a blanket beside my family's large vegetable garden

The love of planting and harvesting is in my DNA.

while Mom tended to the plants that would fill the family's larder for winter. I know my love for gardening stems from this early exposure, but I also know that for many generations, the Mennonite moms in my family tree gardened like their life depended on it. The love of planting and harvesting is in my DNA.

The gardens of my childhood had seemingly endless rows of peas to pick, corn to hoe, and raspberries to prune. The chores were backbreaking, the weeding never-ending. In contrast, Grandma's garden, although no less functional, was smaller and more fun. The borders of rosebushes created the sense of a magical land, and as I carried the galvanized watering can back and forth from the water pump to the garden, my imagination ran wild and free, and a love of gardening took root in my very soul.

✦ ✦ ✦

Currently we tend over 8,000 square feet of garden every summer and preserve more than five hundred quarts of food from it. Our garden is large because our growing season is short and intense from May 15 through September 15. This gives us a one-shot chance at most crops and little to no room for do-overs with those long-season crops. But even with the intensity of the short growing season, gardening brings a joy that feels more like a hobby than a chore. The early morning weeding while the plants are wet with dew, picking strawberries that are warm from the sun, and even the backbreaking labor of hoeing feel like a form of worship when I realize I am working alongside my Creator to bring forth a harvest that will nourish the family.

Whether you're a beginner or a seasoned gardener, whether you are growing for fresh eating or for preserving, whether you are inspired by the health benefits of organically grown crops or the visual beauty of a garden, I hope to inspire you to find a deeper connection with your Creator through gardening.

GROWING YOUR GROCERIES

The full-size gardens of the Amish and Mennonite communities are breathtakingly beautiful. Long, tidy rows of vegetables stretch from border to border. Families work together to grow bushels of food for winter. I can spot a Mennonite or Amish homestead during my travels merely by the design, size, and layout of their garden. Gardens are a cultural influence in those communities because everyone gardens the way their parents did and builds upon the mistakes and successes of the generations before them. These generational gardeners are not easily influenced by trends or fads but rather are focused on production.

Just like the homesteaders who have gone before, production is what inspires me to garden. The garden fits into the priority of nutritional well-being for the family, and therefore, caring for it is near the top of my chore list almost every day during the growing season.

Although we are a few generations removed from the intensity of the Depression-era gardens, I still like to garden in a way that fills our larder to the brim and makes an immense difference in our monthly grocery bill.

Growing What You Eat

What to grow? Studying your shopping list is the first step toward deciding what to grow in your garden. If you see frozen peas, canned green beans, or pasta sauce on your list every month, then you have a good idea what to start growing. You will save money, and the health benefits of eating homegrown veggies are priceless.

When you are holding your list of groceries up to your garden plot, the idea of growing things like grapes, raspberries, or peaches can feel overwhelming when you consider that those crops take years to establish before you get a return on your time and investment. While I would encourage you to begin your perennial garden as soon as possible when you start your homestead, many annual garden plants, potatoes, tomatoes, and beans are just as impactful on the family's diet and grocery bill.

Eating What You Grow

An important part of creating the right family garden equation is adjusting your family's diet to reflect what you can grow in your region. Where I grew up, it was easy to grow peaches. Every neighbor seemed to have bushels and bushels of sweet, juicy peaches in baskets beside the road with a "for sale" sign perched on top. Peaches were a large part of my childhood diet, as Mom canned hundreds of quarts or more each summer. Now raising our own family in the cold and snowy upper Midwest, it took me quite a few years to accept that I would not be canning peaches; any peaches we can get are shipped, expensive, and lacking in flavor. Instead, we preserve and eat the fruit that we can grow, including apples, pears, sour cherries, plums, and of course a few kinds of berries.

All this fruit, when it is grown organically here on the homestead or by local farmers and then picked and preserved at peak ripeness, supplies my family with more nutrients than any fruit that has been chemically treated, harvested in an unripe condition, and shipped from faraway states. We count any fruit or veggies that have to be shipped in as a special treat and not as part of our yearly nutritional needs. Adjusting your diet to match what you can grow is a significant way to reduce costs and eat healthy.

Without a lot of effort, we can grow corn and beans by the bushel here in Iowa. Peas, however, prefer a more acidic soil and don't produce as well. This merely means corn and beans are our everyday fare and peas are special-occasion fare. If your family is like mine, it's best to make changes toward "eating according to what we can grow" in small ways that eventually add up to make a big difference over time.

GROWING LOCAL

Gardens vary greatly from region to region. Not only are climates extremely different, but the growing seasons and types of soil also play an important role in how you should approach your choices. For this reason, I am not going to get into the minute details of what to plant or when to plant because this information, based on my experience, would only be relevant to readers in my growing zone and surrounding areas. Instead, I encourage you to find a garden mentor within your area.

Visit your town's farmers market and find a gardener who grows crops in abundance, and they should be able to answer questions for you or at the very least connect you with local gardening resources. Also, many colleges and universities have extension programs for agriculture and gardening information and can provide help as well as training and resources.

SOURCING THE BEST SEEDS

Although all seeds are created with a tiny miracle inside waiting to spring forth with life, not all seeds will germinate. The careful gathering and storing of seeds is an art that fascinates me. Although I do save some seeds from my garden every year and store them in my freezer to protect them from the temperature and humidity changes that negatively affect the germination rate, I purchase most of my seeds for our big crops, including corn and beans.

When sourcing your seeds, make sure you're buying from a licensed seed company that is inspected by the USDA. What this means is that they have run required germination samples of their seeds and are required by law to print the percentage of germination rate on their packages. They take a sampling of seeds from each variety and germinate them. If enough seeds from that variety germinate to fall into the government's required rate of germination for that crop, then the seed company can package them. The seed company then stores them in a temperature- and humidity-controlled warehouse that is also regulated by the USDA.

So, what happens to all the seeds that don't meet the required germination rate? They are boxed up and sold to big box stores where unsuspecting gardeners buy a package of fifteen green bean seeds, plant them with hope, and get a total of four to five bean plants. Then discouraged, the gardener blames their own lack of skill and experience, never once suspecting that the $2.99 package of seeds never had the potential to grow what was desired.

UNDERSTANDING COMPOST AND MULCH

Compost is organic matter that has been broken down to a point where it has a similar consistency to soil. It is used to amend—improve—soil and has readily available nutrients for plants. Compost is not an effective weed barrier.

Mulch is any material, organic or nonorganic, that is placed on top of the soil as a weed barrier and also as a moisture and temperature stabilizer. The soil then does the work of breaking down the organic matter into compost. Mulch does not contain readily available nutrients.

Organic mulches are composed of things that were formerly living, such as wood chips, straw, grass clippings, leaves, and pine needles. Nonorganic examples are cardboard, newspapers, black plastics, and fabric-type ground covers.

In our garden we use organic mulches that then compost and help amend our soil just like compost would.

To successfully use organic mulches as compost, you need to have a basic understanding of the composting process. When you place organic matter like fresh grass clippings or wood chips on top of the soil, the microorganisms in the soil begin to break down the mulch, much like the body digests foods. These tiny microorganisms, while working to compost the mulch, utilize the same nutrients that your plants need in order to grow strong and healthy. This means that during the composting process, this soil has far fewer nutrients available to give your plants.

The deeper the organic matter is incorporated into the soil before it is fully composted, the more nutrients that become unavailable

to our crops. Crops that are planted where organic matter/mulches have been incorporated into the soil will struggle to thrive and produce. It is better to leave organic mulches undisturbed on top of the soil. This knowledge is where the popular and trendy "no till" method of gardening stems from. And while the no-till method is successful, tilling is not all bad. You will be a much better gardener if you merely understand where and when to till and when to avoid it.

Since we know that only the soil that is in direct contact with the organic matter is lacking nutrients, we understand that available nutrients lie just below that surface. Although climate and precipitation play a role in how fast organic matter will compost, generally speaking, the lighter the organic matter is, the easier it is for the soil to compost, the shorter the amount of time it will take, and the shallower your nutritional deficiencies in the soil will go.

Two ways we keep nutrients available to our crops while still using organic mulches:

1. We wait to place organic matter on the soil until crops are established and their roots are extending well down into the soil.

2. We place the coarser and harder-to-compost organic matter around the crops that have a deeper root system.

Organic Mulch

Our favorite organic mulch is grass clippings, which are readily available to us. Every week we can collect four to five wheelbarrow loads of grass clippings from our organic yard. We are mindful to gather them and place them on the garden while they are fresh and green, and we pile them on no less than six inches deep because the moisture in the fresh clippings combined with the depth will cause them to compost. The heat from the composting process will effectively sterilize any weed or grass seeds that we may have collected and also insulate the soil, giving my crops a boost.

Grass clippings compost easily and completely in a few weeks, making them the perfect weed barriers for all my short-season shallow root crops like radishes, lettuce, and brassicas such as broccoli and cabbage.

My longer-season deeper root crops like tomatoes, peppers, and squash get chunkier organic matter like a partially composted manure/hay/straw combination that we collect from the barn stalls.

And the only place I use wood chips as mulch is on perennial crops like fruit trees and bushes that have very deep root systems that reach down far below the nutritional deficiencies caused by the slow-to-compost wood chips.

Nonorganic Mulch

Fabric and plastic mulches are popular among commercial growers because they can control the amount of moisture and nutrients their crops get, leading to more consistent crops. Because fabric and plastic won't compost and add nutrients to the soil like organic compost does, regardless of how long you leave it in place, you will need to fertilize your crops to ensure they are receiving the proper nutrients. And because these types of mulches block most if not all rain from falling onto the surrounding soil, you need a watering system to go along with them.

Because nutrition is my number one motivation for a garden, I shy away from plastic and fabric mulches, and I don't want to use synthetic fertilizers and well water. Instead, I want the micronutrients that fall with the rain and the nutrients from organic mulches to feed and nourish the plants that will in turn feed and nourish my family.

In 2020 and 2021, inspired by empty spots on the grocery store shelves and talks of food shortages, people set out to garden with all the vigor of their Depression-era ancestors. My brother and my sister, both who own and operate retail greenhouses, sold vegetable plants like never before. My Mennonite neighbor who sells garden seeds was selling out of seeds every week and struggling to keep her shelves stocked. And now a few short years later their sales have all settled back into the average range. This leads us to believe that most of these new gardeners didn't continue to garden past that first

year. As an experienced gardener, I can offer a few guesses as to what happened:
- Weeds were continuous and discouraged the gardeners.
- Blight or pests diminished the harvest, to the point the work didn't seem worth the effort.
- The extra cost in their water bill surprised them.
- It was more work than they expected.

In short, they had expectations from their garden that far exceeded their experience or the effort they were willing to put in.

One thing you can always expect the garden to cost you is time—time spent preparing the soil, time spent tending the plants, and time spent harvesting and then preserving. But over many seasons of investing time in the garden, you gain so much, including experience, confidence, and knowledge.

GROWING CONFIDENCE AND CHARACTER

> Over many seasons of investing time in the garden, you gain so much, including experience, confidence, and knowledge.

Sometimes at the end of the season when you put the garden to bed for winter, you may feel like you've created a deficit. The time and effort don't reflect the return in the way you expected. But gardening cannot be reconciled in one season alone. It may take years of gardening before you can reconcile all the time and effort with the impact on your family's nutrition and budget. If you stick with it, one thing your garden can produce that cannot be measured or assigned a price tag is the legacy of skills you are teaching to and values you are instilling in your children and grandchildren. You are planting seeds of influence that could certainly benefit future generations.

A season that seems to have been a total loss because of weather, disease, or pests should never be despised. In such years you harvest the most experience, develop the muscle of endurance, and refine your knowledge. To build your knowledge right away, this chapter closes with more helps and tips.

My hope is that you will stay encouraged. Gardening calls you to invest in long-term goals and be future-sighted with your plans. Similar to your parenting journey, gardening requires patience and many seasons of mistakes and adjustments to build confidence and feel successful and prosperous. When looking back over ten or even five years, you will see the abundance of not only the bushels of food you have grown and preserved but also the knowledge, skill, and character that has been developed in the gardener.

HOW TO START A NEW GARDEN

In the fall, measure out your plot, keeping in mind that a small, well-tended garden will often yield a bigger harvest than a larger, neglected, and weed-challenged garden.

Cover the entire area with cardboard or several layers of newspaper.

On top of the cardboard or newspaper, add a layer of compost six to eight inches thick. Organic matter such as grass clippings, leaves, old hay, or partially composted manure work too; you will just use a different approach in the spring when planting.

In the spring, the cardboard will have composted and you will have a beautiful garden ready for planting. Be careful not to disturb the soil more than absolutely necessary in new gardens, as weed seeds will lay dormant for up to seven years waiting for a chance at some sunlight.

If you used organic matter instead of compost, I recommend using seedlings instead of direct seeding the first year. Plant your seedlings deep down into the soil where the nutrients are. In the fall or next spring when the organic matter has fully composted, you can use the direct seeding method.

I have successfully used this method to revitalize an especially weed-prone area of our garden.

Gardening calls you to invest in long-term goals and be future-sighted with your plans.

TREATING AND PREVENTING BLIGHT AND FUNGUS

Blight is a common disease in backyard gardens and is often aggravated by the fact that gardeners love to water, and blight- and fungus-type diseases love moisture.

Blight is best prevented by making sure not to water more than necessary. However, you are not in control of how much precipitation falls from the sky, so sometimes you need to take actions to treat the blight that is sure to follow a rainy season.

BLIGHT PREVENTION TIPS FOR TOMATOES

As soon as the tomato plant is firmly established and has multiple branches, remove the lower branches to prevent them from hanging onto the ground. Blight and disease live within the soil, and your plants contract them from the soil.

In addition to removing the bottom branches, consider placing a layer of mulch (we love grass clippings for this) over the soil to prevent soil from splashing onto the tomato plants during rain showers.

MILDEW PREVENTION AND TREATMENT FOR PLANTS

We use the following recipe as a preventive treatment on all susceptible plants like squash and pumpkins. I've also successfully used it to treat and prevent the spreading of powdery mildew in my zinnia garden.

DIRECTIONS

Mix water and peroxide together. With a heavy mist, spray this mixture onto plants that have visible signs of blight and onto those that are susceptible.

The peroxide will kill existing spores and prevent spreading of the disease.

I apply this every seven to ten days during wet weather as a preventive measure. I spray in the evening as the sun goes down to give the peroxide time to work overnight before the sun has a chance to evaporate it.

INGREDIENTS

1 gallon water

½ cup 3% peroxide (or 2 tsp. 35% peroxide)

DEALING WITH PESTS IN THE GARDEN

Nothing is more disheartening than being forced to share your garden with hungry pests with six legs, enormous appetites, and millions of offspring.

Science tells us that unhealthy and struggling plants emit different pheromones than healthy plants and that insects are more attracted to the pheromones of struggling plants. This information reinforces my experience that your best line of defense against insects is to nurture healthy soil that will give your crops a solid chance at growing healthy and vigorous.

The timeline for planting is important in your battle against pests because in most cases the insects that are detrimental to the crop will hatch when the soil or air reaches a certain warm temperature. If you've planted your crop into healthy soil as soon as it was possible, you've given your plant plenty of time to grow strong and be able to withstand the effects of the insects once they hatch, without negatively affecting your harvest.

Inevitably, you will find pests in your garden. Don't go looking for pests and panic over every insect. Many insects, even harmful ones, live in a delicate balance within the ecosystem of your garden. And by treating for one insect, you are often harming many beneficial insects and risking the upset of this ecosystem.

We rarely, if ever, treat for insects but rather focus instead on supporting the crop that is host to the insects with micronutrient fertilizer much the same as we would support the human immune system when it contracts a virus. In this way, we are encouraging the plants to grow vigorously and survive the life cycle of the insects and still go on to produce a harvest.

When we do treat an area, we use diatomaceous earth (food grade) sprinkled generously over the affected plants. (Never use DE on or around plants with blooms because it will also kill your beneficial pollinating insects.)

NATURAL BUG REPELLENT FOR PLANTS

DIRECTIONS

Mix and spray onto brassicas to deter cabbage worms; this also works on other plants to deter aphids.

Before I treat crops for insects, I weigh the risks and benefits. Is this a crop that my family depends heavily on for winter meals? If no, then I usually decide not to treat it. If yes, then is there a chance I can simply support the crop and give it time to outgrow the damage? If this is possible, I don't want to treat it and risk further upsetting the balance of insects in my garden.

INGREDIENTS

1 T. peppermint castile soap

1 quart water

Potato Beetles

These are easy to see and therefore easy to pick off the plants. It takes my children less than an hour each day for the duration of three to four weeks to pick off all the potato beetles they can find. Getting paid one penny for each bug and two pennies for each leaf with eggs on it keeps them motivated. They have earned a nice amount of money to deposit into their bank accounts with this simple job.

Japanese Beetles

I bank on the fact that my neighbors will put up traps for Japanese beetles in their yards, where the scent of the dead beetles will attract all the beetles from my yard, giving me a minimal problem with these bugs. However, some do remain in my garden and, again, most of my plants are vigorous and healthy enough that although you can see the effects of the beetles, these insects don't diminish the harvest. When I see more than the occasional Japanese beetle on a crop, I take action. I fill a cup with soapy water and go early in the morning when the dew is heavy and the beetles can't fly, then I stealthily knock the beetles into the cup of soapy water where they drown without ever emitting the odor that attracts more beetles to the yard.

Whenever you are collecting bugs in water, don't forget to add some dish soap to the water because it breaks the surface tension of the water, causing the bugs to drown.

Harmful insects are as much a part of my garden as the beneficial insects are, and sometimes the solution for me has been as simple as switching to a seed variety that is more resistant to the effects of insects.

Modern hybrid varieties of veggies are often cultivated with the assumption that the grower is willing to use pesticides to grow a successful crop. Understanding that your style of gardening may be better suited to the "more disease and pest resistant but not so pleasing to the eye" plant varieties is a huge step toward being a successful gardener! Other times, the solution has been to choose a different time of the season to plant a crop and in this way avoid the damage of the insect to my harvest. Brassicas, for example, when planted six to eight weeks (by direct seed) before our first frost, will form an outstanding and worm-free harvest because the cabbage worms all die with the first frost.

Varmints: Raccoons, Voles, Moles, and Rabbits

Rodents and similar pests like to operate under the cover of darkness, their antics hidden by the night. In the morning when the gardener arrives, smile on her face and steaming cup of coffee in hand, she is disappointed at the damage they have done in one short night.

These creatures have shown up in my garden often, and although I have tried many different methods to deter them, the most successful one has been to use human hair clippings or dog hair from clippings or brushings. Place the hair generously along the rows of crops that the varmints love most, and even press the hair into the tunnels and hills of underground varmints such as gophers, voles, and moles.

Once upon a time when I had only one little boy with blond ringlets that I hated to trim, I had rabbits visiting my garden and nibbling at my pea sprouts. At first I ignored it, thinking, *I have a hundred feet of peas, I don't mind sharing the end of one row with a*

rabbit. But yes, you guessed it, that rabbit brought his bunny family, and before long they had nibbled twenty-five feet of tender pea sprouts right down to the ground. What to do? Sacrifice the curls of my firstborn son to save the pea crop? I decided to save the curls and visit the neighborhood barbershop to ask for hair clippings. I launched into this long story about rabbits in my garden and how my son didn't really need a haircut but I needed hair clippings to deter the rabbits, thinking there's no way I could ever show my face in this barbershop again after this confusing ramble. But much to my surprise, the barber grabbed a shopping bag, a broom, and a dustpan and filled the bag with hair for me. With a smile he said, "Oh, I do this too. And I just filled the bag with clippings for another gardener this morning."

As the story goes, I went on to add three more sons to my family and four more dogs and have never again needed to take a humbling trip to the barbershop.

The underground varmints have been the trickiest of all for me. Although pet and human hair stuffed into their tunnels does seem to deter them, the only real cure for them that I've noticed is snakes. When we had the worst gopher and vole issue, I noticed how the bull snakes moved in, and in one season the underground varmints were gone. So now when I see the bull snakes, although I don't think I will ever not scream, I try my best to embrace them as a part of the beautiful cycle of my garden.

Rodents and similar pests like to operate under the cover of darkness, their antics hidden by the night.

CHAPTER FOUR

FILLING THE LARDER

Preserving the fruits of your labor

Harvest day is a busy one. The garden harvest days of my childhood involved every sibling of working age and usually both my parents as well. The seemingly endless rows stretched out before us. We worked in pairs, an older, more efficient sibling working next to a younger, less skilled child. The pressure to get the harvest preserved was felt by all. As a child, I assumed Mom just wanted to get the job checked off the list. But now, as a gardener and preserver myself, I understand the precise timing was to preserve as many of the nutrients and as much of the taste as possible.

In my life as a homesteader, I excitedly prepare the soil and carefully plant, tend, and nurture the plants until they bless me with fragrant blossoms. Then, burdened with fruit, they droop in a posture of worship, begging me to harvest their bounty. Hand in hand with the Creator, I work through this season to bring forth the fruit I stare at, awed by its beauty and a touch intimidated by its intelligent design. The reason I pause is because I am fully aware that as soon as I remove the harvest from the life-giving branches, I activate the enzyme within the fruit that begins the composting process and therefore initiate the race between my preserving efforts and the composting efforts of the enzyme.

My goal is to capture the nutrients of these fruits when they are at their peak.

You see, as far as the plant is concerned, its only reason for bearing fruit is to ensure the survival of its kind. When the fruit is fully ripe, the core softens and the plant releases the fruit onto the ground where this enzyme begins composting the flesh, leaving the seeds to lie in a nutrient-dense bed of compost where they then sprout and repeat the cycle. This is the intelligent design that I want to interrupt. My goal is to capture the nutrients of these fruits when they are at their peak, just before the plant would naturally drop the harvest, to provide for my family during the long, cold months of winter.

I carefully plant, tend, and nurture the plants until they bless me with fragrant blossoms, and then, burdened with fruit, they droop in a posture of worship, begging me to harvest their bounty.

To capture and preserve these nutrients is not an easy task. It requires many hours of being trapped in a hot kitchen on an already hot summer day. I have been known to proclaim many times that gardening is my first love and preserving the harvest is just the price I must pay for my love of gardening. Over the years, though, and no doubt with a bit of maturity, I've been able to extend my love of the garden to include the jobs of harvesting and preserving. This shift has taken my love for growing things and turned it into a full-scale passion that also has a purpose—to serve my family many economical and nutritious meals over the years.

A WELL-TIMED HARVEST

When you reach your very first harvest, it takes great discipline to resist picking the fruits of your labor too early! We want to pile it up in baskets and set it on our countertop and gaze at it lovingly much like a mother regards the face of her newborn child. We can't wait to show it off and enjoy it. But alas, if it has been picked, then we must be making a plan to put it into jars.

So whether you are harvesting bushels of fruits and veggies at a time or a few bowls full, it is wise to have a plan for the harvest before you pick it. Many a bushel of harvest goes to waste because the gardener, seeing that the fruit was ripe, harvests it without next steps in

FILLING THE LARDER   99

mind. It is better to leave the fruit on the plant where it is naturally preserved while you clear your schedule and gather your supplies for the long-term preservation of the harvest. Then when you are ready, you get up early and harvest your crop while the dew still rests upon it. Daytime heat turns sugar content into starches, and the nighttime dew converts these starches into sugar. Preserving the harvest with the highest sugar content results in the best taste, texture, and nutrients, so always harvest in the morning.

Tomatoes

I know many gardeners pick their tomatoes before they are ripe and allow them to ripen in a cool, dry place. This practice has been adopted from commercial growers who like to wash, package, and ship their tomatoes while they are still hard and green to ensure that they arrive at the supermarkets with little to no damage. Once you taste the difference between your home-canned tomato products where you allowed the tomatoes to ripen on the vine versus the tomatoes that ripened off the vine, you will become a believer.

The only time I pick tomatoes that are unripe is if our first frost is imminent and I still have tomato products that I want to preserve. But during most summers I gladly anticipate that first frost because I am so tired of canning and preserving and am ready to throw all remaining produce to the pigs anyway! Another popular method

Preserving the harvest with the highest sugar content results in the best taste, texture, and nutrients.

of harvesting tomatoes is to allow them to ripen on the vine and then collect them in the freezer until you have accumulated enough or have the time to preserve them. I don't see a problem with this method at all except as it relates to my personality. I'm very much of an "out of sight, out of mind" person, so there is trouble come early winter when we harvest our beef and pork and need the freezer space occupied by the tomatoes that September RuthAnn didn't deal with!

Sweet Corn

Delicious sweet corn has a high sugar content, therefore it is important to harvest this crop at the right time. If you harvest too early, the sugar content will not have developed and you will have flat-tasting sweet corn. In contrast, if you harvest too late, the kernels will be too mature and the sugars will already have converted to starch, leaving you with an unpleasant tacky texture.

The best way to tell if sweet corn is nearing ripening is to watch the silk on the cob change color. It will go from a white blond to a pink shade and then to a brown color. When the silk is brown, I peel back the husk and take a peek at the cob. If the rows of kernels are all filled in, pressing against each other from the bottom to almost the top, then I know it is ripe and ready to harvest.

If you're growing corn for fresh eating, the taste and texture may not be as big of an issue, but when you preserve corn, whether in the freezer or through drying or canning, the flavor and texture are magnified.

When buying sweet corn from a grower, be sure to ask for corn that has been picked that morning and stored in the shade. And purchase only the amount that you can preserve within that same day.

Onions

You can tell an onion is ripe when the stems fall over. This means the bulb has reached maturity and is now taking nutrients from the stems into the bulb, which causes the stems to weaken and fall over. If your soil is not saturated with water, you can leave onions to cure in the dry soil for a few weeks after the stems have fallen over. Otherwise, harvest them right away and then cure them by spreading them out on a table in a cool, dry place out of the sun to allow the skins and necks to dry and seal out moisture. Once the skins are dry and paperlike and the necks are tight and dry, you can pile the onions into baskets to store in a cool, dry place for the winter. Some onion varieties will store much longer than others. If you want to store onions for winter, make sure to plant a "storing" variety such as yellow globe or sweet Spanish.

Garlic is in the same family and will give similar signs of maturity. When the scapes (seed heads) appear, remove them, and then a few weeks later you will see the browning of the foliage begin. When two to four of the bottom leaves are brown, it's time to harvest, cure, and store your garlic the same way you did your onions.

If you don't have a cold room, a dark closet will do. Humidity, light, and moisture are the enemies of stored potatoes.

Potatoes

Potatoes are also a root crop, so the signs of maturity are similar to those of garlic. The beautiful plants that you are so proud of will suddenly start looking yellow, and you may think they are blighting. But really all that's happening is the plant has reached maturity and is beginning the process of pulling the nutrients from the foliage into the roots, which are your potato crop. And although you can harvest potatoes for fresh eating anytime you can find them under the plants, harvesting them for winter storage should be done only after the plants are completely dead.

After harvest, spread potatoes out in a cool, dark, and dry place for a few days to allow the skins to properly cure before piling them into baskets for storage in a cold room. If you don't have a cold room, a dark closet will do. Humidity, light, and moisture are the enemies of stored potatoes.

Fruits

Most fruits are ripe when they are easily removed from the stem. This happens because as the fruit ripens, the internal chemistry of the fruit changes and its hold on the stem weakens. Observing your fruit harvest closely over a few seasons will help you learn when different varieties are ready. Strawberries that are perfectly ripe can be easily plucked from the plant and their core removed easily. Ripe raspberries will simply drop into your hands when you give them a tiny tug.

Although wind and rainstorms can cause apples to drop prematurely, I watch to see when apples start dropping naturally. If the tree increases the number of apples it drops each day, then I know it's likely time to pick them all. But because the weather varies so greatly from year to year, it is not possible to mark my calendar and say, "The first week of October is when this variety will be ready to harvest." Although the calendar and your experience can give you an idea when to expect your harvest, watching for dropping apples will give you the best indication of timing.

Pears are tricky because they release from their stem a few weeks before the flesh is sweet and ripe enough for eating. We always have a better harvest if we pick the pears green and allow them to ripen in the cold room, separating the pears with newspaper to keep them from touching and spoiling each other.

Experience is the best teacher of all, and mistakes are where we learn the most. How did I learn to harvest the pears weeks before they're ripe? Because one year we lost almost an entire harvest when they all dropped, bruised, and rotted before they were ripe. Lean into your harvesting mistakes, embrace them, and learn from them. When mistakes are made, there are only two possible routes to take: give up, or try again with adjustments.

GETTING PRIME PRODUCE FROM GROWERS

Not everyone has the time or space to plant, grow, and tend the size of garden that will give them bushels of produce to preserve for winter. Thankfully, there are many resources available where growers and preservers can connect! A CSA (community supported agriculture) program is a great resource. My favorite is the local farmers market where I was once a vendor way back when my love of gardening was still bigger than my family's consumption of garden goods. I had two toddler girls at the time and was only able to work between their naps. We grew as many veggies as we could and then picked, washed, and packed them into plastic tubs and loaded them onto a trailer. We strapped the girls' car seats onto the trailer with a ratchet strap, hitched the trailer to our tractor, and drove the three miles to our small town to sell the veggies!

You want produce that was picked that same day.

It was a great way for me to help make our mortgage payment while doing something I loved. Eventually our family grew, and it wasn't long before every crop I had the time to grow and harvest went straight into jars for our personal winter meals.

Whenever you are purchasing the harvest from a grower, it is best to make sure that you can purchase the product as soon as possible after it was harvested. Most growers are out in their fields at sunrise to avoid the heat of the day, picking their produce before the sun turns those sugars to starch. They will understand when you want to stop by to pick up your order well before noon. You want produce that was picked that same day. Don't purchase from the piles of produce that have been sitting in the sun all afternoon; rather, ask to fill your order from the veggies that are stored in the shade. Sunshine on picked produce quickly breaks down all the good stuff.

As for refrigerated produce, I personally don't purchase refrigerated produce for canning purposes unless the price is extremely economical or, as in the case of peaches in Iowa, I'm purchasing a small amount to preserve as a treat for wintertime.

CANNING TIPS

Be careful when ladling a hot mixture into glass jars. If they are cold, it can cause the glass to break from the temperature difference. I make sure my jars are at least room temperature before filling them with hot mixture.

Always remove rings from your jars before storing, as rings can create a false seal, hiding the fact that a seal has gone bad and the product should be thrown out. Rings can also rust onto the glass jar, making it difficult or impossible to open your jar.

Never double-stack home-canned goods, as the top layer of jars can put pressure on the lids of the bottom layer and cause the seals to let loose. If you must stack, place a thin layer of wood or sturdy cardboard between the layers to evenly distribute the weight of the top layer of jars.

HOW TO BE A HAPPY CANNER

To take the fear and mystery out of canning your garden produce with simple and easy family favorite recipes, I'll first explain the difference between pressure and water bath canning.

Water Bath Canning

What is water bath canning? When a jar of a high-acid product is immersed in boiling water until the product is heated thoroughly, your product, as it cools, creates a vacuum. The heat of the water bath and hot product softens the rubber of the lid, the vacuum pulls it down, and the lid seals onto the rim of the jar. The vacuum creates an absence of oxygen, thus preserving the product by preventing oxygen-loving bacteria from growing.

Products that are precooked, such as applesauce and pasta sauce, only need to be processed in a water bath long enough to thoroughly heat the product in the jar so that when the jar is removed, the temperature difference as it cools is drastic enough to create a vacuum.

Example A: I like to cook my sauce and salsa in a large pot without a lid for forty-five to ninety minutes to evaporate any excess liquid. This way these sauces thicken without having to add thickeners.

This means that when I process my sauces in a water bath, they are already fully cooked and all possible bacteria is destroyed, and I need only to heat them thoroughly to create a vacuum and soften the rubber.

Example B: If I were to juice my raw tomatoes and put that juice into the jars, I would need to process those jars in a water bath for forty-five to sixty minutes to thoroughly cook the juice in the jars.

For fruit like peaches, pears, and cherries, we raw pack them (put them into jars raw), then add a couple tablespoons of sugar and fill the jar with warm water. Next, we process in a water bath for five minutes—just enough to seal the jar. The fruit doesn't have to be cooked, just preserved. The high sugar content of the fruit, the added sugar, and the lack of oxygen from processing prevents bacteria from growing. Any longer than five minutes and you will have fruit mush instead of nice, firm slices of fruit.

❖ ❖ ❖

Pickles are another product that does not need to be cooked. The vinegar and sugar create an extremely high-acid environment that, combined with the lack of oxygen in a sealed jar, is enough to preserve your cucumbers. A maximum of five minutes processing in a water bath is my rule for preserving the crispiest pickles. My favorite is three minutes of a rolling boil.

High-acid products that can be preserved by water bath processing:

- Fruits
- Pickled veggies
- Jellies
- Jams
- Tomatoes
- Tomato salsa and sauces if they contain added acid like vinegar, lemon juice, or citric acid

Pressure Canning

What is pressure canning? It's when a jar of low-acid food is heated under pressure to bring the temperature to 240° and higher for a certain amount of time. The amount of time required is determined by the density of the product. This time and high temperature are necessary to kill the bacteria botulinum that is responsible for the botulism spore.

Unlike other bacteria, *Clostridium botulinum* can live in low to zero oxygen environments, deep under the soil, in rivers and seas. If botulinum bacteria were to be present on the veggies you are preserving, then the low-oxygen, low-acid environment of the sealed jar would be the perfect place for this bacteria to grow and give off the toxic botulism spores. This is why pressure canning is needed for low-acid foods.

Low-acid foods that should be pressure canned:

- Asparagus
- Beets
- Carrots
- Green and dried beans
- Okra
- Peas
- Peppers
- Potatoes
- Pumpkin
- Sweet corn
- Beef and poultry
- Seafood
- Wild game
- Meat sauces
- Soups and stews

FUN FACT

I grew up canning and eating canned food and never even knew there was such a thing as botulism. Not until I created a social media account and started watching people can and preserve did I hear the word, and because of the fear that surrounded botulism, I made a point to learn about it. Fear is only the symptom of not understanding something as well as we would like to. I was relieved to discover that botulism from foodborne cases is quite rare, and cooking the food you have pressure canned will also destroy any possible botulism spores. I was also happy to learn that of the few reported cases of botulism in the United States each year, only a small fraction are foodborne cases and that a healthy immune system will often deactivate the spores before a body is aware of a problem.

PASTA SAUCE

Makes approximately 7 quarts or 14 pints

DIRECTIONS FOR TOMATO JUICE

Wash, core, and quarter tomatoes and cook until they are soft, then run through a food mill to remove skins and peels.

Alternately: Wash and core tomatoes; toss into a high-powered blender and puree into juice.

DIRECTIONS FOR SAUCE

For a chunky sauce, finely chop the onions and peppers and add to the juice with herbs and remaining ingredients.

For a smooth sauce, blend herbs and veggies (cooked or uncooked) in blender with some of the juice. Add olive oil, tomato paste, sugar, salt, garlic, and seasonings to your tomato juice mixture.

In a heavy-bottom stockpot, simmer all ingredients together, uncovered, until sauce reduces and is thick to your liking. The normal range would be 1 to 3 hours. Stir frequently, making sure to scrape the bottom to keep sauce from scorching.

Ladling hot mixture into cold glass jars can cause the glass to break from the temperature difference. I make sure my jars are at least room temperature before filling them with hot mixture.

Ladle pasta sauce into clean, hot jars. Wipe clean the rims, place lids on jars, and turn rings finger tight. Process in a hot water bath for 10 minutes.

We use this sauce as a marinara sauce, pasta sauce, and pizza sauce.

TIP: Low-Acid Ingredients

Tomato sauce and salsa recipes often include low-acid ingredients like peppers and onions that can lower the overall pH of the sauce. Therefore, it is a precautionary step to add an acid ingredient like vinegar.

INGREDIENTS

1 gallon tomato juice (from about 12 to 15 lbs. whole tomatoes)

1 to 2 large onions

2 bell peppers

1 handful fresh basil leaves, chopped (or 1 tsp. dried)

1 handful fresh oregano leaves, chopped (or 1 tsp. dried)

½ cup olive oil

1 to 2 cups tomato paste (increases pH and helps thicken)

½ to 1 cup granulated sugar

¼ cup salt

1 clove garlic, minced

Optional seasonings:

1 T. Italian seasoning

2 tsp. parsley flakes

2 tsp. pizza seasoning

1 to 2 bay leaves (remove before canning)

CHILI BASE

Makes approximately 7 quarts or 14 pints

DIRECTIONS FOR TOMATO JUICE

Wash, core, and quarter tomatoes and cook until they are soft, then run through a food mill to remove skins and peels.

Alternately: Wash and core tomatoes; toss into a high-powered blender and puree into juice.

DIRECTIONS FOR CHILI BASE

Coarse-chop veggies and puree them in a blender with a couple cups of your tomato juice.

In a heavy-bottom stockpot, mix pureed veggies and tomato juice. Add the remaining ingredients and simmer for 30 to 45 minutes.

Ladling hot mixture into cold glass jars can cause the glass to break from the temperature difference. I make sure my jars are at least room temperature before filling them with hot mixture.

Ladle chili base into clean, hot jars. Wipe clean the rims, place lids on jars, and turn rings finger tight. Process in a hot water bath for 10 minutes.

To Prepare Chili:

In a large pot, combine:
- 1 quart jar chili base
- 1 quart jar tomato juice
- 1 pound browned ground beef
- 1 quart jar canned baked beans
- Spices, to taste

Adjust flavors by adding salt, cayenne pepper, or other favorite spices and simmer on the stove until heated through and you have the depth of flavor you desire.

INGREDIENTS

- 6 quarts tomato juice (from about 18 to 20 lbs. whole tomatoes)
- 2 green peppers
- 1 large onion
- 1 cup vinegar
- ¼ cup chili powder
- 1 T. black pepper
- 3 T. salt
- 1 tsp. cinnamon
- 1 tsp. allspice
- 1 tsp. ginger
- 1 tsp. dill weed
- Optional: 2 hot peppers or 1 T. crushed red pepper

SALSA

Makes approximately 7 quarts or 14 pints

DIRECTIONS

In a large, heavy-bottom pot, mix all ingredients together. At this point you have pico de gallo, so make sure you dish some out and enjoy it!

Leaving the pot uncovered, bring the salsa to a fast simmer and cook until some liquid has evaporated and the salsa starts to thicken. This will take approximately 45 minutes, depending on how juicy your tomatoes were or how well you strained them.

If you feel your salsa remains too thin and you want to thicken it, you can use 5 tablespoons ClearJel, ThermFlo, or Perma-Flo dissolved in 1 cup cool water. Mix until smooth and add to your boiling salsa; stir well until incorporated. Boil for another 5 minutes.

Ladling hot mixture into cold glass jars can cause the glass to break from the temperature difference. I make sure my jars are at least room temperature before filling them with hot mixture.

Ladle salsa into clean, hot jars. Wipe clean the rims, place lids on jars, and turn rings finger tight. Process in a water bath for 10 minutes.

INGREDIENTS

4 cups finely chopped tomatoes, strained well (no need to peel them or remove seeds)

3 cups finely chopped onion

1 cup finely chopped bell peppers

½ cup finely chopped jalapeño peppers or any hot peppers (remove seeds for mild salsa; include seeds for hotter salsa)

½ cup apple cider vinegar

½ cup chopped cilantro

3 cloves garlic, chopped or minced

3 T. salt

1 T. chili powder

2 tsp. cumin

Optional: 1 to 2 T. granulated sugar

HAMBURGER DILL PICKLES

Makes 7 quarts or 14 pints

DIRECTIONS

For the crispiest canned pickles, harvest your cucumbers before they are fully mature. A mature cucumber will have smooth skin and fully developed seeds in the center. An immature cucumber will have puckered skin and a solid center with underdeveloped seeds. The immature cucumber will stay firm and crisp after canning.

Cut your clean cucumbers into ¼-inch slices. Stuff them into 7 clean quart-size jars, making sure to settle the cucumbers firmly into the jars by firmly thumping each jar on a hard surface. (I place a potholder onto my table and thump against that.)

Into each quart jar, add:
- 1 clove garlic
- 1 head fresh dill seed or ½ tsp. dried dill seed
- ¼ tsp. turmeric
- 1 bay leaf

Halve these ingredients if you are canning in pint jars.

In a heavy-bottom stockpot, boil the water, vinegar, and salt until the salt is dissolved. Pour this mixture into the jars full of sliced cucumbers, leaving 1 inch headspace. Wipe clean the rims, place lids on jars, and turn rings finger tight. Process in a hot water bath for 3 minutes.

The processing time for pickles is short for a few reasons: The vinegar keeps bacteria from growing, and the pickles don't need to be cooked to be preserved. You only need to heat the product enough to soften the rubber and create a vacuum, therefore sealing your jar.

INGREDIENTS

40 to 50 young cucumbers

7 cloves garlic

7 heads fresh dill seed (or 3½ tsp. dried dill seed)

1 ¾ tsp. turmeric

7 bay leaves

3 quarts water

1 quart white vinegar

1 cup salt

SWEET DILL PICKLES
Makes 7 quarts

DIRECTIONS

Divide the sliced cucumbers, garlic, and dill evenly into 7 clean quart-size jars. In a heavy-bottom stockpot, make brine by boiling the water, vinegar, sugar, and salt until the sugar and salt are dissolved. Pour this mixture into the jars full of sliced cucumbers, leaving 1 inch headspace.

Wipe clean the rims, place lids on jars, and turn rings finger tight. Process in a hot water bath for 3 minutes.

INGREDIENTS

40 to 50 young cucumbers

14 cloves garlic

1 tsp. dill weed

2 quarts water

2 quarts white vinegar

6 cups granulated sugar

4 T. salt

PICKLED BEETS

Makes 7 pints

DIRECTIONS

Cut off the beet tops, leaving 1 to 2 inches of the stems attached. Scrub the beets to remove any garden dirt.

Put clean beets into a heavy-bottom stockpot and cover with water. Cook until beets are soft like a boiled potato but not falling apart.

Strain off the juice and save it for your brine. I like to strain mine through a fine cheesecloth.

Cool your beets with cold water until they are cool enough to handle, and then peel them. The skins should be loose enough to simply rub them off.

While waiting for beets to cool, make brine. In a large saucepan, boil 2 cups of the beet juice with the vinegar, sugar, and salt until the sugar and salt are dissolved.

Slice the beets into ¼- to ½-inch slices. If my beets are larger than baseball size in circumference, I will cut the beet in half before slicing.

Divide cooked beets evenly into 7 clean pint-size jars. Pour brine evenly into the jars full of sliced beets.

Wipe clean the rims, place lids on jars, and turn rings finger tight. Process in a hot water bath 8 minutes for pint-size jars and 10 minutes for quarts.

INGREDIENTS

6 cups cooked, sliced red beets (from about 7 lbs. whole beets)

2 cups beet juice (from cooking your beets)

2 cups white vinegar

2 cups granulated sugar

1 T. salt

DRY CANNED POTATOES

Makes approximately 7 quarts

DIRECTIONS

Peel and dice potatoes into approximately 1-inch pieces, cover with cold water, and let sit for 4 to 6 hours; then drain and rinse them. This removes some of the starch and helps keep the texture integrity. Pack potatoes firmly into 7 clean quart-size jars, making sure to settle the potatoes firmly into the jars by firmly thumping each jar on a hard surface. Leave 1-inch headspace at the top.

To each jar of potatoes add:

- 1 tsp. ghee or butter
- ½ tsp. salt
- ¼ tsp. black pepper

Wipe clean the rims, place lids on jars, and turn rings finger tight. Process in a pressure canner for 45 minutes at 10 pounds pressure.

Create a classic homestead breakfast by tossing a jar of these potatoes into a hot cast-iron pan with a bit of butter or bacon grease, fry until they're crispy outside, and then serve with a side of over-easy eggs and some bacon or sausage links. Delicious!

Why go through the process to can potatoes when they are a crop that holds up well in cold storage? Convenience! Canned potatoes are a quick, easy meal addition. We often use them in place of frozen hashbrowns. For canning, we select potatoes that wouldn't store well, such as tiny ones and those with blemishes or cuts from harvesting.

INGREDIENTS

5 to 8 lbs. Russet potatoes (or a similar variety)

Ghee or melted butter

Salt

Black pepper

PINEAPPLE ZUCCHINI
Makes 7 pints

DIRECTIONS

Stuff diced zucchini into clean pint jars. To each jar, add 2 tablespoons of granulated sugar and 2 tablespoons of lemon juice. Fill the jar to 1½-inch headspace with pineapple juice.

Wipe clean the rims, place lids on jars, and turn rings finger tight. Process in a water bath for 25 minutes.

Although zucchini and squash are low acid and should normally be pressure canned, the acid in the pineapple juice and lemon juice increases the acidity enough to process in a water bath.

INGREDIENTS

5 to 7 (8- to 10-inch) zucchini or summer squash, peeled and diced

14 T. (almost 1 cup) granulated sugar

14 T. (almost 1 cup) lemon juice

46 oz. 100% pineapple juice

PIE FILLING
Makes 7 quarts

DIRECTIONS

In a heavy-bottom stockpot, bring water, sugar, and salt to a boil until sugar and salt are dissolved. Use the full amount of sugar for tart fruit like sour cherries and less sugar for sweet fruit like peaches, apples, or blueberries. Meanwhile, slice larger fruits into the size of slices or chunks you prefer in your pie.

Mix the ClearJel into the 2 cups cold water and whisk until dissolved. Add ClearJel mixture to the boiling sugar water and stir well, bringing back to a boil while stirring; the mixture will get thick very fast. After mixture is thickened, remove from heat and add fruit, making sure to stir all the way to the bottom of the pot.

Ladling hot mixture into cold glass jars can cause the glass to break from the temperature difference. I make sure my jars are at least room temperature before filling them with hot mixture.

Ladle pie filling into 7 clean, hot jars; I like my wide-mouth jars for pie filling. Leave 2 inches headspace, as the raw fruit will expand when you can it.

Wipe clean the rims, place lids on jars, and turn rings finger tight. Process in a water bath for 20 minutes.

Variations:

Apple Pie Filling: Add 2 T. cinnamon

Blueberry Pie Filling: Add 2 T. lemon juice

INGREDIENTS

6 cups water

4 to 6 cups granulated sugar

1 tsp. salt

4 to 6 quarts raw fruit, washed

2 cups ClearJel, ThermFlo, or Perma-Flo

2 cups cold water

What is ClearJel?

ClearJel (not Sure-Jell) is a modified corn starch that is heat stable and doesn't break down and become runny when reheated like many other thickeners do. Also sold as Perma-Flo or ThermFlo.

NO-PECTIN JAMS
Makes approximately 5 pints

How did Grandma make jams and jellies if she didn't have pectin? She knew that fruit contains its own naturally occurring pectin. All she needed to do was activate the pectin by adding some sugar to the fruit and heating it. Sugar helps activate the natural pectin, so the more sugar you add to the fruit, the shorter amount of time you will have to cook it. You can add lemon juice or finely chopped green apples (or apple cores) to your fruit during the cooking process as an added source of pectin.

INGREDIENTS

2 quarts mashed fruit or fruit juice

2 to 4 cups granulated sugar, to your taste preference

DIRECTIONS

If using peeled, chopped fruit, you can put it all in the blender and make a puree before you add the sugar and begin the cooking process.

If you have a fruit with skins and seeds like grapes, cook the grapes with a bit of water until they are soft and have released their skins and seeds, run them through a food mill to remove the skins and seeds, then use the thick juice to begin your jam process.

For raspberries (or other fruit with tiny seeds), cook the raspberries with a bit of water until they've released their seeds and then strain them through a fine cheesecloth, squeezing to make sure to get as much of the flavorful pulp as possible. Or if you and your family aren't sensitive to tiny seeds, just mash the fruit, add some water, and leave the seeds.

Add your sugar to the mashed fruit or fruit juice (add a bit of water if necessary) and simmer gently until mixture coats the back of a spoon. Different varieties of fruit will contain different levels of naturally occurring pectin and will require more or less simmering time. When the jam coats the back of a spoon, do a cold plate test (directions to follow) to see if it sets.

To do a cold plate test, put a plate into the freezer for a few minutes, remove it, and drop a few drops of your boiling jam onto it and see if it "sets" or if it "runs." If it runs, continue to simmer for 5 more minutes and then test again.

If it sets, you are ready to ladle the jam into clean, warm pint jars. Wipe clean the rims, place lids on jars, and turn rings finger tight. As the jam cools it will create a vacuum and seal the jars. If your jars are smaller than a pint or you have pints that didn't seal, process them in a water bath for 10 minutes.

APPLE OR PEAR BUTTER
Yield varies

DIRECTIONS

Apple and pear butter are made just like no-pectin jams and jellies except they are cooked longer and develop more of a caramelized taste.

I chop my apples or pears (if they are not homegrown or are badly blemished, I peel the fruit too), put them in the Crock-Pot with half the amount of sugar as I have fruit (I always go light on the sugar because I can add more later if I want to), turn the Crock-Pot on low, and go about my other work all day long. Depending on how full your Crock-Pot was, you will cook the apples or pears between 4 and 8 hours. Taste periodically and add more sugar if you want a sweeter butter.

When the fruit and sugar have cooked together into a golden mash, you know it's ready! I then take my immersion blender and puree the mixture.

Ladle apple or pear butter into clean pint jars, wipe clean the rims, place lids on jars, and turn rings finger tight. Process in a water bath for 5 minutes to get a good seal on the lids.

To speed up the process, start with applesauce or pear sauce in place of raw fruit.

INGREDIENTS

Apples or pears

Granulated sugar, to taste

◆ CHAPTER FIVE ◆

PIGS, POULTRY, AND PLANNING
Embracing the learning curve

It's the very early 1990s, I am still a few years from becoming a teenager, and I am dressed in a homemade dress and apron with two long braids of blonde hair falling down my back just like every other Old Order Mennonite girl in the community. I am headed to the barn to milk our family's milk cow, who stands patiently in her stall next to our buggy horses. Anxiety grips my heart as I try my best to carry the stainless-steel milk bucket without the tiniest bit of sound. I am fully aware that with the slightest clang of the handle, I risk entering the most chaotic race to bring milk to the house that you could ever imagine. You see, we had a barnyard pig named Henry who was always on the watch for fresh milk.

Henry was one of hundreds of pigs on our farm, but what made Henry different was that he was a runt and was therefore able to squeeze through the gates that kept all his siblings and relatives contained. What Henry lacked in size he made up for in cunningness. And hunger drove him to extreme measures.

What Henry lacked in size he made up for in cunningness.

What began with a taste of warm milk splashed into the cat food dish after each milking quickly became Henry's addiction. Here there was no competition from his littermates, and Henry quickly figured out the routine with the family milk cow. What was initially endearing literally grew into a hundred-pound milk-crazed monster. My siblings and I were no match for Henry, and time after time he chased us down, got his strong snout over the rim of the bucket, and buried his face into the warm, frothy milk all the way up to his eyes! Our frustration would bring us to tears. Mom eventually got fed up with all the buckets of milk that she was missing in the kitchen, and Henry left the farm with the next load of pigs that my family sold.

Now, more than thirty years later, as I share Henry-the-runt stories with our children, the former tears of frustration are now tears of laughter. And I understand my father's amusement at our ingenious but thwarted attempts to save the day's milk. This heritage of learned wisdom and crazy antics while caring for animals is priceless.

The animals you bring onto your homestead will keep you on your toes.

The animals you bring onto your homestead will keep you on your toes and, of course, provide a lot more than humor. They are in your care for a reason—to help provide for your family and possibly others. Whether you have a wide range of livestock or one pig and a chicken, you are the steward of these animals. Planning for how to best care for them allows you to get the best from them. Your growth—and theirs—will be a memorable journey during which you'll gain confidence, know-how, and more than a few good stories to share around the family table for years to come.

MAKING A HOME FOR YOUR ANIMALS

A lot of frustration can arise when we try to fit animals onto the homestead without asking how we can make a functioning home for them. Turkeys are going to roost in the rafters, and their droppings are going to go everywhere. Pigs are going to push around loose feed troughs and spill open water. Steers are going to test boundaries and know when the fence isn't electrified. And ducks are going to splash in water wherever they can find it. Making choices and task lists for the farm is easier when we accept that we won't change the animal's

nature; we must adjust our expectations and plan accordingly.

Assessing what your homestead has to offer before you decide to bring animals onto it is a step that shouldn't be bypassed. You can of course bring a cow home without having pasture and shelter available, but you will spend more money on feed and will have some unpleasant milking experiences when the weather is bad. But nothing inspires someone to build a pasture faster than the monthly feed bill. In the same way, having to milk your cow in the icy rain will motivate you to build a shelter pronto. Maybe your homestead has mostly woodland, and you really want a milk cow. Fencing the woodland and purchasing pigs and goats for clearing would be a logical first step toward getting a milk cow.

There are no hard-and-fast rules for homesteading. Sometimes the opportunity to bring an animal home happened first and then our love and care of that animal inspired us to build the shelter and acquire the resources needed. Other times we've acquired animals and then remodeled existing structures to fit their needs after we learned about the animal's nature and habits. We have been able to shave years off our self-sufficiency plan by being okay with using makeshift and temporary plans for animals; then once we decide the animals will become a permanent part of the homestead, we spend the time, money, and effort to make that happen. A couple dozen steel T-posts, a spool of wire, an electric fence charger, a salvaged plastic tub, and a water hose were all we used to create a home for our first cow. The land we fenced in was mostly ragweeds and nettles, and the fence wasn't pretty and required much upkeep, which is usually the case with minimal investments. It was our quicker way to have a family milk cow.

Now when we make changes, we put more thought and effort into them. We have set our focus further into the future and are making decisions about where to place water lines and install permanent fencing. However, don't be afraid to make cheaper, short-term plans with the knowledge that the personal experience you'll gain will serve you when making long-term plans and investments.

In the case of our pigs, Elvin and I both brought experience to the game. However, that made us overconfident in our skills. We didn't pause to consider that our lack of proper equipment would be a challenge. We eventually made it work using some creative troubleshooting, which I'll share in this chapter.

Again and again, ingenuity as well as trial and error become as important to the homestead experience as the physical tools you have in your barn or shed.

WEE, WEE, WEE ALL THE WAY HOME

Making choices and task lists for the farm is easier when we accept that we won't change the animal's nature; we must adjust our expectations and plan accordingly.

When we brought home Petunia Pig and her barrow brother Pumba, they left the livestock trailer and took off at a full run through their new woodland pasture. They had been separated from their herd and taken for a ride in a rattling trailer and were understandably scared out of their minds. My heart sank as I watched them disappear into the woods. I worried that they wouldn't see the fence on the far side and would run straight through the electric wire. I also knew that at the speed they were running they would be able to make it through the fence in between zaps of electricity. Fortunately, Pumba felt the electricity and turned back. Petunia, on the other hand, made it through undeterred and was headed for the vast Iowa cornfields at a dead run. Fortunately, when she realized that her brother was no longer beside her, she turned around and ran right back through the electric fence to join him. She felt the jolt and began her education on electric fences.

Because of my childhood experience with Henry and many other pigs, an electric fence was at the top of the list of things we did to prepare to bring home our first pigs. We already knew that an electric fence is the only kind of fence that a pig will truly respect, but we didn't know that a pig must be trained to respect an electric fence.

On three sides of our woodland pig pasture, we had a woven wire fence. This served as a barrier that would physically stop the pigs. Inside that woven wire fence, we ran a strand of electric wire. This is exactly the kind of fencing needed to retain pigs for any length of time. Because a pig with its strong snout will eventually dig under any physical barrier, the electric strand is needed to keep a pig from ruining the barrier.

The problem with the fourth side of our pig pasture was that it bordered the cow pasture, which was a high tensile fence consisting of four to five strands of high-carbon steel wire stretched tightly between wooden posts. These types of fences are very strong and are often used to contain large livestock like cows and horses. They work very well to contain large animals even when not electrified.

Our education on containing pigs on the homestead didn't end there.

When we brought home a weanling boar late the next summer, we again learned a lesson. Porky fit into a large dog crate, and we left him in one with food and water out in the barnyard for twenty-four hours. That's because once an animal has been fed in a place and has slept there, they have a sense of home. Their instincts will have them return there in the event of an escape.

This little boar, new to the herd, was treated like an outsider. Petunia and Pumba made sure to let him know he wasn't welcome, and within minutes he escaped through that high tensile fence and

TIP: Hot-Wire Training for Pigs

Create a small paddock using a visible physical barrier with a single strand of hot wire along the inside, approximately eight inches from the ground. Once a pig is trained to respect the hot wire, you can keep him contained in a much larger area with a single strand of hot wire. Pigs don't accept strangers into their herd. When adding new stock, separate them with a fence to allow them to get to know each other for a few days before incorporating newcomers into the herd.

into the vast soybean field across the road. Ten days later, after we had given up hope of ever seeing him again, he returned to the last place he remembered being fed and watered—the barnyard!

TRAILER TRAINING 101

I promised you a tale of creative troubleshooting for raising pigs. We learned a big lesson on harvest day. We don't butcher our pigs here on the homestead. Instead, we load them up in a trailer and take them to a Mennonite butcher shop in the community.

The spine and neck of a pig are extremely strong. This amazing structure gives their snout the power of a small bulldozer. A full-grown sow can lift the side of a car without any problem. This anatomy also means that pigs cannot lift their heads very high at all, so it is most unnatural and difficult for a pig to go up steps. You can probably guess where this story is going by now. It's butcher day, and we have five three-hundred-pound yearling pigs to load into a trailer. There are jobs and school to get to and we all wait, yet the pigs refuse to step up the twelve inches into the trailer. Their noses stay down on the ground, and no matter how hard we push, shove, and crowd them, they refuse to budge. After more than an hour, when they have exhausted all of us and pushed Elvin and me to the brink of divorce and the children to tears, one hog finally steps onto the trailer and discovers the milk in the trough that we have had there all along to entice them. The sound of his slurping gets the attention of his siblings. They lift their noses up over the edge of the trailer and, with lots of force and encouragement from behind, we finally get them onto the trailer.

After the dust settles, Elvin is off to work and the children to school. I'm on my way to the butcher shop with the five pigs in the trailer, thinking about all that went wrong, and suddenly all the special hog loading equipment that we had on the hog farm of my childhood makes perfect sense—the special trailer with hydraulics that allowed it to drop to ground level and the long narrow loading chute that slanted ever-so-slightly upward. The loading chutes were

so narrow that once a hog entered the chute, there was no room for it to change its mind and turn around. I had the humbling realization that mere experience isn't enough. At the end of the day, when the family was smiling again and all the harsh words uttered in the morning had been forgiven, we faced our options:

1. Invest in better loading equipment.
2. Butcher the hogs ourselves (approximately the same amount of investment in butchering equipment).
3. Exclude pigs from our homestead lineup.

The garden and kitchen waste they consume makes up for their cunning and stubborn personalities.

By now, our sow had another litter of piglets, so we were too invested to change our minds on raising pigs. Besides, we had all developed an extreme fondness for homegrown, heritage breed pork!

As butcher day for the next litter was fast approaching, we needed a solution. I came to Elvin with a plan. I reminded him of my childhood experience with Henry and his addiction to milk and suggested, "What if we parked the livestock trailer in the pig pasture, put troughs with milk into the trailer to entice the pigs, and trick them into becoming comfortable with boarding the trailer?" After all, Henry had crossed all types of obstacles to get to his warm milk, so surely our pigs weren't so different and would happily jump even eighteen inches to receive the frothy, satisfying reward.

Thankfully, my theory was correct. After a few weeks, the now half-grown piglets were standing at the gate squealing in anticipation of their liquid meal and jumping into the livestock trailer without hesitation. When harvest day arrived, all it took to load five fat hogs in under a minute was a bit of warm milk.

After our initial learning curve, we have found pigs to be easy to raise. The garden and kitchen waste they consume makes up for their cunning and stubborn personalities. Knowing how our pigs are raised and where our favorite ham comes from continues to give us peace of mind and amazing, quality meals.

RAISING POULTRY

Often my thoughts turn to my childhood and the ways I learned about homesteading from my family. I think back on a day when Grandpa and Grandma arrived in their horse and buggy right after breakfast. But unlike many of their visits, there was no time for visiting on this occasion—it was chicken butchering day! Dad and Grandpa got the fire started under the scalding cauldron while Mom and Grandma filled tubs with cold water. With no fancy plucking machines available to us, it was instead an all-hands-on-deck kind of plucking party. The scalded chickens were strung up by twine, and we worked in pairs all morning to get the plucking done.

After the chickens rested in the cold water and we had some lunch, we went straight to eviscerating—the removal of the chickens' internal organs. Grandma tried her best to make the task educational, taking her time explaining everything and showing us the lungs, the gizzard, the liver, and the heart. Yet, despite her best efforts, I was too squeamish about it all to take much of an interest. My entire education in chicken butchering happened mostly because of my desire to be close to Grandma.

Although chicken harvests have gotten easier with modern inventions like electric plucking machines and vacuum sealers, modern-day RuthAnn still finds poultry harvest day to be one of her least favorite days of the entire year. This is also why we stick to raising the fast-growing and larger Cornish Cross chickens, of which we only need thirty birds to harvest two hundred pounds of meat.

Meat chickens require a lot of work, but once we saw and tasted the difference between chickens raised indoors and those raised in pastures, we decided to find a way to make it work regardless of my dislike for the project. One summer we stumbled upon a trick that has made raising meat birds easier. In the layer house, I had a couple broody hens that would've loved nothing more than to hatch out a clutch of chicks. So I put them in the brooder with the one-day-old meat birds, and they promptly went to work mothering the

chicks. The chicks' instincts took over too. They started following the broody hens and snuggling under their wings. This made a big difference in the behavior of this batch of meat birds. The Cornish Cross birds are not known for their foraging skills or ability to find shelter in bad weather, but this batch—raised and taught by their adoptive mamas—could forage for bugs and seek shelter better than any previous ones.

We've used variations of this method over the years. Because we don't always have broody hens at the same time we get baby chicks, we decided to place a few grown hens in with the chicks when we moved them from the brooder to the chicken tractor. This also made a difference in the Cornish Cross birds' ability to forage. When harvest day comes for the meat birds, the laying hens move back to the hen house, their nannying jobs complete.

We were looking for a way to have homegrown poultry without the intense six to eight weeks of raising the Cornish Cross, feeding, watering, and moving the chicken tractor (a mobile chicken coop), and that is when turkeys entered our homestead. While visiting a farm in our area, we learned about heritage breed turkeys and how hands off and economical they are to raise for a poultry source. The

FIND THE RIGHT BREED FOR YOU

Sometimes the solution to a problem animal is as simple as trying a different breed. When adding ducks one year, we didn't expect them to be so messy and noisy. However, the eggs were far superior to chicken eggs when it came to making homemade pasta. We have learned that the Muscovy breed of ducks is a better fit for our homestead since they are neither as messy nor as noisy as the Pekin breed that we first tried.

We had the same first experience with the family milk cow. We originally chose a Dexter cow because we wanted a smaller cow that would be easier for me to manage. But it turns out that the good nature of a Jersey was a better fit for me than the sassiness of the Dexter, and the size difference wasn't a big issue after all.

farm raised their turkeys as free range and had a nest or two of poults each summer that the family harvested in the fall. I was inspired as soon as I heard "free range." This meant that the turkeys raised themselves! Plus, each turkey was the size of two chickens.

We left that farm with a dozen turkey eggs and promptly put them into our incubator. Unfortunately, only one of the twelve eggs hatched, but the good news was that the egg hatched on the same day that one of our broody hens hatched out her chicks, and the lone turkey, which we named Uno, was adopted by this broody hen and raised as a chicken! Uno grew up with the chickens, and it was quite comical to see the large turkey try to snuggle up under the wings of her adoptive mama chicken.

Uno has gone on to be a wonderful mom and raises her clutches without any help from us now, free ranging them all over the property all summer long. Our Narragansett hen, Juliet, has still to figure out how to successfully hatch a clutch, and our tom, Romeo, proudly rules the barnyard around here and is the first to alert us when something unusual is going on.

When we walk away with knowledge that we didn't have before, then experience is gained, and when we build upon each experience, even when the outcome isn't what we expected, we are growing as homesteaders.

Romeo proudly rules the barnyard around here.

EGG NOODLES (HOMEMADE PASTA)

Serves 6 to 8

When the chickens were laying eggs with abandon and the yolks were as yellow as the sun, then it was time to stock the pantry with egg noodles. I cut this recipe down from the twelve dozen eggs in the original recipe from my grandma to make it a one-meal recipe and to save you from having pasta invade every flat surface of your home like it did in the days of my childhood.

INGREDIENTS

1½ cups all-purpose flour

1 tsp. salt

3 to 4 large egg yolks (or 2 whole eggs)

3 T. water

1 tsp. fat (melted butter, lard or tallow, or cooking oil)

DIRECTIONS

Mix flour and salt, then add egg yolks or eggs, water, and fat.

Mix by hand until dough comes together in a nice ball, adding more water or another egg yolk if necessary. Continue to knead for 8 to 10 minutes until the dough is soft and a bit stretchy. Wrap in plastic wrap and let rest at room temperature for 2 hours or in the refrigerator for 4 to 8 hours.

Roll dough as thin as you can, let it dry for 30 to 60 minutes, and then roll it up, jelly roll style, and cut thin strips off the end (or use a pasta machine).

Cook the strips in broth or water for 8 to 15 minutes (depending on how thick or thin you rolled your pasta) until pasta is tender to your liking.

Alternately, when pasta is cut, you can let it dry until it is crisp and breaks easily and then store for up to 6 months in your pantry.

ROASTED WHOLE CHICKEN
Serves 10 to 12

DIRECTIONS

Combine your spices in a small bowl, then rub them over the outside of the chicken, except if starting with a frozen chicken (see directions below for frozen chicken).

Roasting options:

To cook in a Crock-Pot, place breast side down and cook on low for 7 to 8 hours. (No need to add water. The chicken will make its own juice.)

To bake in oven, place seasoned chicken with the breast side up in a large roasting pan and add 2 quarts of water. Bake at 350° for 3 to 4 hours, turning to breast side down halfway through.

If you start with a frozen chicken (like I usually do):

Place 2 quarts hot water and your frozen unseasoned chicken into your roasting pan with the breast side up. Bake at 400° for 2 hours. Remove and add the spices to the chicken, turn it breast side down, and return it to a 250° oven for another 3 to 4 hours.

INGREDIENTS

4 tsp. salt

2 tsp. lemon pepper

2 tsp. paprika (I like smoked paprika)

1 tsp. onion powder

1 tsp. black pepper

½ tsp. garlic powder

1 whole chicken

HAM AND BEAN SOUP

Serves 10 to 12

DIRECTIONS

Sauté celery, carrot, and onion in butter. Add your broth. If you have less broth, add water to bring your liquid to approximately 3 quarts of liquid. Add salt (less salt if your broth and ham are very salty), pepper, and potatoes. Cook until potatoes are soft. Add the ham and beans. Simmer for 30 to 60 minutes to allow the flavors to incorporate.

INGREDIENTS

2 to 4 ribs celery, chopped

1 large carrot, shredded or chopped fine

1 small onion, chopped fine

3 T. butter

3 quarts ham broth (or at least 1 quart broth and add water)

2 tsp. salt

2 tsp. black pepper

4 to 6 large potatoes, diced

1 to 3 lbs. leftover ham, chopped into small pieces

15 to 30 oz. precooked great northern beans

THANKSGIVING AMISH ROAST

Serves 8 to 10

This recipe is an alternative to stuffing that is often used for large family gatherings and weddings in Mennonite and Amish communities. I find it a good way to use leftover chicken or turkey any day of the year. I also save all my less-than-perfect bread slices and end pieces in the freezer for recipes like this.

DIRECTIONS

Place bread cubes, chicken or turkey, and onion into a 9 × 13-inch pan. In a medium-size bowl, whisk eggs and milk, then add seasonings and schmaltz. Pour egg mixture over bread and chicken. Cover and bake at 350° for 45 to 55 minutes or until knife inserted in center comes out clean.

INGREDIENTS

8 cups bread cubes

3 to 4 cups finely shredded chicken or turkey

1 small onion, chopped

6 eggs

4 cups milk

2 T. dried parsley (or ⅓ cup fresh)

2 tsp. salt

2 tsp. dried sage (or ¼ cup fresh)

4 T. schmaltz (or butter)

RED BEET EGGS (PICKLED EGGS)

Serves 12

Red beet eggs were prominent in my childhood, and now I understand why. Eggs pack a powerful nutritional punch, and having multiple ways to serve them to the family helps me offer variety while not compromising nutrition.

DIRECTIONS

Hard boil your eggs: My favorite method is to bring a pot of water to a boil, use a spoon to carefully add refrigerated eggs to the water, and boil for 10 minutes. Drain off the water and plunge the eggs into an ice bath. Peel once eggs are completely cooled.

Into a medium-size bowl, put your hard-boiled eggs and pickled beets, making sure all the eggs are submerged in the liquid. Cover and refrigerate.

After 24 hours the eggs are ready to eat and will only get more flavorful with time. Keep in refrigerator for 7 to 10 days, submerged in beet juice.

INGREDIENTS

1 dozen eggs

1 quart pickled beets (page 124)

MOM'S PUMPKIN PIE
Makes one 9-inch pie

Though this recipe doesn't relate to pigs and poultry, I wanted to provide you with a yummy dessert to go with the Thanksgiving Amish Roast. Personally, I hesitate to try a pumpkin pie unless my mom or one of my sisters has made it, simply because my mom's pumpkin pie is my favorite—not so full of spices that you can't taste the pumpkin and not so bland that it tastes like a savory dish.

DIRECTIONS

Set out the pie shell at the ready, then put all other ingredients into blender and blend until mixed and foamy. Pour into pie shell. Bake at 375° for 60 to 75 minutes. I start checking for firmness after 60 minutes. Pies are done when edges are slightly cracked and the middle has a firm rather than sloppy jiggle when you shake them.

Because of the fat content in pumpkin pies, they are great candidates for freezing. As soon as they are cooled, wrap them firmly in tinfoil and freeze for up to a month.

INGREDIENTS

1 (9-inch) pie shell, unbaked

1 cup pumpkin puree (or other squash puree, such as butternut squash)

1 egg

1¼ cup milk

⅓ cup granulated sugar

⅓ cup brown sugar

¼ cup all-purpose flour

1 tsp. vanilla

½ tsp. nutmeg

½ tsp. salt

RUTHANN'S CANNED CHICKEN AND BROTH

Makes approximately 1 quart per carcass

When we harvest our chickens, we part out most of them. This means that after resting the chickens in cold water, we remove the breasts, legs, thighs, and wings and bag them up separately for easy use in winter recipes. What we are left with is what I call the carcass. The meat that remains on the carcass is the back and neck meat and any meat that was left by our less than professional parting job.

On harvest day I bag the carcasses 4 to 6 per bag (throwing a couple chicken feet into each bag for broth purposes) and save them in the freezer. In the fall, I pull out one or two of these bags and create a delicious broth. Here is my go-to process:

DIRECTIONS

Fill a Crock-Pot or electric roaster with chicken carcasses. Add enough water to cover approximately half of your chicken.

Set the heat to 250° (low) and cook the carcasses, covered, for 24 hours from frozen or 12 hours if using thawed carcasses. Strain the carcasses from the broth and begin the job of removing all the pieces of meat. Into clean quart jars, put approximately 2 cups of meat in each jar, and fill the jar with broth, leaving a 1-inch headspace.

(I always have more broth than I need for my jars of chicken, so I can the extra broth in jars alone, without any chicken.)

Wipe clean the rims, place lids on jars, and turn rings finger tight. Process the jars of chicken and broth in a pressure canner for 45 minutes at 15 pounds of pressure.

INGREDIENTS

Chicken carcasses with meat

Water

CHICKEN NOODLE SOUP
Serves 10 to 12

I use my canned chicken and broth to make many winter meals of chicken noodle soup.

DIRECTIONS

Gather your carrots and celery from the garden. Clean the vegetables and dice or slice them to your preferred sizes.

In a heavy-bottom soup pot, sauté the vegetables in a bit of butter. When the vegetables have softened, add the chicken and broth with additional broth if desired, and bring to a boil. Stir in the pasta and seasonings, and simmer until the pasta is tender. Then serve the perfect meal for a cold, dreary winter day!

I add a quart of corn to any leftover chicken noodle soup to make another complete meal for us later in the week.

INGREDIENTS

Carrots

Celery

Butter

1 quart canned chicken and broth

Additional broth, to taste

Homemade pasta (page 153)

Salt and pepper, to taste

GRAVY
Yields 1 cup

Instead of packaged gravy mixes or premade gravy in cartons, you can make your own.

DIRECTIONS

Pour your broth into a small saucepan over medium heat. Add salt and pepper and bring it to a simmer.

In a separate small bowl, mix the water and flour until smooth (I like to use a drink shaker for this, but a wire whisk works too). Stir the flour mixture into the broth and simmer until thickened, stirring most of the time.

INGREDIENTS

1 cup broth

1 tsp. salt, or to taste

¼ tsp. pepper, or to taste

¼ cup cold water

2 T. all-purpose flour

CHAPTER SIX

QUEEN OF THE HOMESTEAD
Appreciating the family milk cow

The morning sun is just peeping over the horizon as I walk to the pasture, stainless steel milk pail in one hand and a cup of cooling coffee in the other. The family milk cow, Brenda, waits patiently for me at the gate, lazily chewing her cud and keeping rhythm to some unknown cow tune with her swishing tail. I relish this time alone in the morning, just me and the cow and the early sounds of the pasture and the woods around us. The routine is so familiar to both of us that as the music of the milk entering the bucket fills the morning air, Brenda's long lashed eyes begin to close in contentment, and my mind starts wandering as the foam in the bucket begins to rise.

This is a familiar scene in my life, and it brings me comfort. I'm grateful to have been raised in the old-fashioned tradition of the Old Order Mennonites and taught by my parents how to milk the family cow at ten years old. As an adult and as a parent, I understand how the responsibility to bring milk to the house every morning before breakfast is a gift that keeps on giving for generations. Such chores formed my character. Today, I have the self-discipline to get up early to milk two cows by myself on a Sunday morning and still, with the help of my husband, get the family to church on time. The responsibility instilled in me a

True contentment is not found in the serving of self but rather in the serving of others.

knowledge that true contentment is not found in the serving of self but rather in the serving of others. And my parents showed faith in me by entrusting chores of increasing importance to my care.

Thankfully, I have continued to find peace in the routines the necessary tasks bring to my life. When I head out in the dark of early morning and experience the solitude and serenity of our homestead, gratitude swells up in my heart. My spirit is soothed by the required actions that became second nature long ago. I know I am a part of what matters—my family's health, our homestead's survival, our animals' wellness, and the care of God's creation.

In the beginning, my husband and I weren't sure we would have all the animals that we now do. At the age of twenty-seven, after six years of marriage and two babies, we both became stronger in our faith and leaned into Jesus for everything. We became less consumed with filling our lives with things, experiences, and wealth and far more focused on bringing value to the lives of those around us. As our family grew, so did our focus and clarity. The desire to instill a work ethic and strong values in the next generation became the foundation we built our homestead on. We didn't set out with the mindset of "let's raise all our own food." Honestly, we were too poor to even think of taking on more mouths to feed . . . including animal mouths! But our slow process of adding each animal was motivated

The desire to instill a work ethic and strong values in the next generation became the foundation we built our homestead on.

by our desire to instill some amazing character qualities into our then small family.

To this day, milking the family cow and making the most of what she provides us is an area of family management I take particular pride in. I hope to pass along these skills and the potential peace of homestead routines to my children even if they are convinced, just as I was at their age, that having to milk a cow before breakfast is the absolute worst chore a parent could ask of a child.

IT'S ABOUT MORE THAN MILK

I quickly came to realize that if we had children to raise, we would need to have a family milk cow.

The possession of a family milk cow or two has become about so much more than fresh raw milk for our own family. In the beginning, with our first family milk cow, it was about the milk alone. But I quickly came to realize that if we had children to raise, we would need to have a family milk cow. The family milk cow, God bless her soul, demands consistency from the entire family. This star of the farm requires a routine to our life that my impulsive and scatterbrained soul craves. She brings a consistency to my parenting that the family needs. They, of course, don't know it, but it's the truth.

When life gets busy and our routines are messed up, there is at least one point, sometimes two, when everyone knows exactly what to expect. Milking time! The chores surrounding the family milk cow are shouldered like a familiar yoke that fits just right. A yoke that has been worn so often that all the pressure points have been worn off and it feels more like a welcome and comfortable routine than a burden. The fact that the cow must be milked no matter how miserable we feel, how unfriendly the weather, or how much whining is happening has not only taught our children to have great endurance but has even taught me to have greater self-discipline.

The very first milk cow we bought is the one that gets the credit for teaching me most of what I have learned about milk cows. We

couldn't afford to buy a cow that was trained and lactating, so instead we bought a yearling heifer right off the range for a few hundred dollars. Smokey was a black Dexter and was as wild as any cow I had ever met. She stood in the far corner of her stall snorting at the sight of humans for the first few weeks after we brought her home.

She slowly warmed to us over the next year, and by the time she calved a year later, I was confident that I had turned her into the docile milk cow of my childhood memories. I was as confident about this as Smokey was about the fact that she did not want humans touching her now swollen and engorged bag. The following weeks were spent in a twice-daily battle with this cow. To this day, I've never met a milk cow able to deliver the swift, accurate, and hurtful kicks Smokey could.

Seeing my body bruised and my tears of frustration prompted Elvin to piece together a milking machine for me. This allowed me to step back out of the way once I had the machine attached and allow the milking machine to take the brunt of the beating for the rest of that lactation.

ESTABLISHING CONTROL OF THE COW

When I am out speaking or responding to those who follow my YouTube channel, I inevitably get questions about establishing dominance with a family milk cow. By the way the people ask, I know they've had their battles in the barn and are growing weary. I've been through that with many milk cows. I tell them as I share with you now that cows establish dominance in a herd by getting other cows to reposition their feet and move out of their way. Therefore, in cow language, if a cow can get you to "move," she is establishing dominance over you. This is especially true when you are in the vulnerable position next to her back legs, because next to her horns (if she has some), those back hooves are her weapon of choice.

When Smokey was able to get me to grab my bucket and move out of the way of her hooves, she was speaking cow language to let me know that she was "boss cow" and I was lower than her in the herd hierarchy. This, of course, was magnified by the fact that she was, at the time, our only cow, and a miniature horse didn't give her the herd dynamic that she needed. Therefore, I was the one who received the brunt of her need for establishing dominance when I showed up to milk her twice a day. A pair of hobbles, a kick bar, and a milking machine is what it took for us to settle into a comfortable relationship during her first lactation. I learned as much about myself, my endurance, and my desire to have a family milk cow as I learned about cows those first couple months with Smokey.

The fantasy fueled by my childhood memories was of me sitting beside a gentle cow as she chews her cud and milk steam rises into my face. The cow's tail swishes over my back and the barn cats rub around my ankles, hoping for a bit of liquid breakfast. The harsh reality was the four-man rodeo that it took to get Smokey from the pasture to the barn, the sound of a small motor running the vacuum pump, and me trying to avoid the flying hooves while attaching the hobble and watching the milk run through plastic hoses into the bucket.

Instead of having a bucket and a strainer to wash, I had a cumbersome number of plastic hoses with awkward cracks and crevices to clean. And although the taste of Smokey's milk was the best of any that we've had here on the homestead, we constantly battled with bacteria counts being high because we didn't have a proper setup for cleaning the milking machine nor did we desire to use the harsh chemicals needed to kill the bacteria that grows on improperly cleaned plastic hoses.

FINDING THE RIGHT COW FOR RIGHT NOW

Even though Smokey's first lactation was nothing like I had dreamt about, we were able to replace store-bought milk with fresh raw milk for our growing family, and this result gave me the confidence I needed as we entered her second lactation. All in all, even though the second lactation went much better, as they normally do, Smokey was clearly not an ideal family milk cow, and we soon started dreaming of a cow that would give us enough milk to replace all store-bought dairy for our family, including cheese, yogurt, cream, and butter.

Being able to replace all store-bought dairy is a much-appreciated bonus of owning a family milk cow.

We wanted a family milk cow that the children could milk. After all, having a family milk cow was about more than providing great nutrition for their growing bodies; it was about helping develop the character of work ethic in the narrow window of opportunity in the rapidly developing minds of our children. We've gone on to have several different family milk cows since Smokey. Some we loved and they loved us back, some merely tolerated us, and some we've had to establish dominance over.

When we have bought new cows, some have checked all the boxes, cost a pretty penny, and were promised by the seller to be our dream cow. Some have come almost as a gift and with little to no promises, while others were sold to us as headstrong and deemed to not be safe around children. But each of the cows we have owned, milked, and loved has had something to offer—whether that's experience, thousands of gallons of milk, numerous calves to raise for meat in the freezer, or gobs of thick and tasty cream. Still others were accepted and loved merely because they were gentle enough for the children to handle.

Whether you are considering the purchase of your first cow, struggling to get along with the third cow you've purchased, have two cows that are eight months into their lactation and you've yet to get a positive pregnancy test from either one of them, or are struggling to treat a persistent case of mastitis, I want you to know that it's all considered part of owning a family milk cow. You haven't failed! When you bring home that first cow, even if she was promised to be everything on your requirements checklist, you are also bringing home the possibility of all the problems that go with family milk cows.

A few things that will make me walk away from purchasing a cow:
- Tiny teats not suited for hand milking (just because that's our primary method of milking)
- History of mastitis
- More than eight months since her last calf and not yet bred back
- Not disease tested

It is wise to assume that your very first cow will likely not be your forever cow. Possibly your second cow will not be your forever cow. But each one will teach you something that will help you become more confident in the skills and resilience needed to be successful.

As the years have passed, my appreciation for the family milk cow has grown significantly. She helps me get the children out of bed morning after morning when I'm tempted to let them sleep in and be slothful well past the hour of decency. She demands the consistency of timely chores that I, without her help, wouldn't be able to muster on a daily basis. In short, she demands the character growth of work ethic in a manner that I couldn't quite manage without her!

Being able to replace all store-bought dairy is a much-appreciated bonus of owning a family milk cow. Cheese, yogurt, butter, ice cream, chocolate milk—the list of blessings is endless when you are bringing three to five gallons of milk into the house each day. And by replacing the store-bought versions with simple homemade versions, you are cutting out countless unnecessary and even harmful ingredients from your family's diet.

✦✦✦

My favorite milk cow memory will always be of when the children, on cold winter days, would fill a cup with a splash of maple syrup and a sprinkle of cinnamon, and impatiently wait for me to finish cleaning one of the cows so they could fill the mug with warm, frothy milk and have the best latte ever.

Now the kids help me with milking each morning; their strong, growing bodies make a big difference in the time it takes to finish chores. All too soon they will be grown with families of their own and the milking will fall to me again. When this time comes, and our need for many gallons of milk lessens, then we will reevaluate our need for a family milk cow. But for now, she is the queen of our homestead. The family milk cow brings a welcome rhythm and nourishment as old as time to all who reside here. Without her and the yearly calves, our grocery bill would be much higher, our meals would lack the nourishment of raw milk and grass-fed beef, and we would be less disciplined as a family. She is the most valued animal on our homestead.

The family milk cow brings a welcome rhythm and nourishment as old as time to all who reside here.

GETTING THE MOST FROM YOUR MILK

During yet another busy season on the homestead, I was immersed in preserving, gardening, and meal planning when suddenly I realized I had a fridge full of old milk. Again. To dump the milk felt extremely wasteful. I had already spent the time and effort on milking chores, and without this hard-earned dairy, I would need to buy cheese and yogurt from the store. The whole point of using my early mornings to milk (or prompt the kids to do so) was to save us money, not cost us more. This repeated dilemma pushed us into problem-solving mode. One of those solutions might surprise you—we decided to add pigs to our homestead. That might not sound like an answer to the surplus milk issue, but it became key to utilizing our cow's milk and saving money in other ways.

I skim the cream from the milk, turn that into butter, and then feed the remaining skim milk to the pigs. This allows me to eliminate butter from my grocery list, and the milk given to the pigs cuts down on their feed costs. A definite win-win for our family.

Learning to use raw milk in your kitchen and daily cooking may require trial and error. Here are my best tips to help you become confident with every gallon of milk you bring to the house.

- Skim cream from milk using a ladle. Wet the ladle with warm water (this keeps the cream from sticking to the ladle) before pushing it right under the surface of the cream and letting the cream run onto the ladle. Store the cream in a clean glass container in the refrigerator for up to seven days.
- Cream turns to butter faster when it is around 60°. When the cream is too cold, it's harder for the fat globules to stick together.
- Raw milk that's clean and chilled immediately will stay fresh for seven to ten days in the refrigerator.
- As milk ages, the naturally occurring lactic acid bacteria breaks down the sugars, so fresher milk will taste sweeter, while older milk will begin tasting tart. We reserve sweet

milk for fresh drinking and tart milk for baking and cooking.
- Use glass or stainless steel for storing milk whenever possible. These materials are less porous and therefore easier to keep sanitary.

RAISING CALVES

When breeding our milk cows, we often choose to use semen from beef bulls. In this way our cows provide more than just milk, they also supply meat for our freezer through their offspring. Because beef takes two years or more to raise to maturity, an investment of time and resources must be considered. That calf is going to be grazing the pasture for two summers and eating hay for two winters before it's mature enough to become a meat source. If you have the resources, raising your own beef from your milk cows is a lovely bonus to owning family milk cows.

When calves are born, we separate them from their mom by placing them in an adjacent stall with a panel that prevents calves from nursing but allows Mom to smell and lick them. We allow Mom to have access to this stall next to her calves until she is no longer interested. The milk we get from Mama is put in buckets and then transferred into bottles to feed the calves. We share the milk with the calves by bottle until they are three or four months old and then gradually wean them.

The milk we get from Mama is put in buckets and then transferred into bottles to feed the calves.

Traditional calf sharing allows Mom and baby to be together for twelve hours and then separate for twelve hours to allow Mom's milk supply to build up. After the twelve hours of separation, Mom is milked and then reunited with her calf. With this method we have found that our cows hold back their milk and cream for their calves and easily develop mastitis. Older calves can tear up the teats with their teeth, making milking time a struggle for us, and weaning time is extremely hard on both cow and calf. Some calves will remember drinking from their mom for months, requiring separate pastures for up to three months after weaning. Although many families have success with traditional calf sharing, we have found our modified version of calf sharing, although more labor intensive for the first few months, to be the most trouble-free in the long run. The most important aspect of calf sharing is that the babies get a belly full of their mama's milk twice a day for the first three or four months of their lives.

◆ ◆ ◆

Watching our cows and calves in lush pasture brings me so much joy, and as I lie in a patch of sunny field and watch them, thanksgiving wells up inside of me. I watch one cow wrap her tongue around a juicy bunch of grass, and with a quick jerk of her head she tears the grass off a couple inches above the roots and works it around to her back teeth where she chews a few times and swallows it. In this way, she quickly fills the largest of her four stomach compartments. Later, as the heat of the day turns the sweetness of the pasture grass into starchiness, she will find a shady spot and get to work chewing her cud, more thoroughly chewing her morning meal.

When she swallows her cud, it will enter a different compartment of her stomach where her body will begin absorbing its nutrients. The fact that she can take the grass that grows so abundantly on our homestead and turn it into highly nutritious milk and meat for our family will be an everyday miracle that I will never tire of witnessing and that will always lead me to a spirit of worship.

BUTTER
Makes approximately 1 to 1½ pounds of butter

Butter is one of my most valued dairy products, and no matter how much milk we dump to the pigs in those "too busy to make cheese" seasons, it doesn't feel wasteful if I've skimmed the cream and churned it into butter.

INGREDIENTS

2 gallons strained, fresh, warm milk

½ tsp. salt

DIRECTIONS

Pour your milk into wide-mouth jars or, for even better access to the cream, pour it into buckets. Chill for a minimum of 2 days to allow all the cream to separate and rise to the top. My favorite time frame is 3 to 5 days. Take a ladle and carefully push it under the surface of the cream, filling your ladle with cream and then emptying it into your churn.

Once collected, allow the cream to sit on your countertop for 3 to 5 hours or until it reaches approximately 55°. Warm molecules move faster; therefore, your 55-degree cream will churn more quickly than chilled cream. You may think that allowing it to heat to more than 55° will give you even faster results, but allowing it to get too warm results in soft, gloopy butter that is difficult to work with.

Churn your butter in a blender, mixer with whisk attachments, or a butter churn until you can see chunks of butter. Many variables affect how much time it will take, including the breed of the source cow, her diet, and the freshness of the cream. Many times I have become impatient with my cream and solved the time issue I was having by stopping the churn and allowing the cream to rest for 30 minutes before restarting. When I have used the blender, the cream sometimes gets too warm, making it necessary to set it into the refrigerator for 15 to 30 minutes before trying again.

Once your cream has churned into little grains of butter, pour the contents of your churn through a strainer placed over a bowl to separate the butter mill from the butter. With wooden spoons or cold hands, start kneading and massaging the butter to help it release the remaining buttermilk. When you feel that you've released all the buttermilk, it is time to rinse your butter under cold water while kneading and pressing it. Next, add the salt and knead a little longer to incorporate it. You've made butter!

BROWNED BUTTER
Yields 2 tablespoons

I am convinced that browned butter has the ability to turn even the plainest dish into a delicacy bursting with flavor. My mother and grandmother both used browned butter generously with their veggie dishes.

DIRECTIONS

Place butter into a small skillet or pot and heat over medium-low heat until the butter turns a golden brown. Use this browned butter to elevate a simple veggie dish, to add perfect flavor to a creamy soup, or to turn eating mashed potatoes into a fine-dining experience.

INGREDIENTS

2 T. raw, homemade butter (or high-quality store-bought)

TIPS: Buttermilk, skim milk, and storage

The more buttermilk you remove, the longer your butter will stay fresh. Any buttermilk that stays in the butter will culture (ferment) and cause the butter to have a sour or tart flavor. When this happens, we merely use the butter for baking rather than fresh eating because it has not truly gone bad, just changed flavor.

We store our butter in the freezer for 12 to 18 months and bring one or two pounds at a time into our refrigerator.

What you have left from making butter is just skim milk, and you can use it as such or you can allow it to sit at room temperature for 1 to 3 days until it is cultured and then use it to make delicious baked goods.

CHOCOLATE MILK
Yields 1 gallon

My family seems to drink gallons of this chocolate milk, and it has filled in the nutritional cracks of many a hurried meal that I have served them.

DIRECTIONS

Mix unsweetened cocoa and hot water until cocoa is dissolved. I like to use a drink shaker cup, but a whisk works too. Then add sugar and mix again to dissolve the sugar. Add vanilla and salt, then add the mixture to milk and mix well. Store in the refrigerator for 3 to 5 days depending on how fresh your milk is. Because this recipe doesn't include the stabilizers that you would find on the ingredients list of store-bought chocolate milk, it will be necessary to mix it up each time before serving.

If you are weaning your family off a store-bought chocolate milk mix, you may need to add more sugar for a while until their palates become accustomed to the lack of corn syrup in this recipe. When my family was adjusting to the homemade chocolate milk, I added a dash of stevia to bring the sweetness level up. (Add stevia to the milk mixture and not to the chocolate syrup, as stevia has a bitter flavor reaction when added to chocolate.)

We use this same recipe for all the hot chocolate we drink in wintertime and just heat the chocolate milk in a saucepan on the stovetop.

INGREDIENTS

½ cup unsweetened cocoa

½ cup very hot water

¾ cup granulated sugar

1 tsp. quality vanilla

Pinch of salt

1 gallon milk (from the barn or from the store, whole, skim, or 2%)

CLABBER (FERMENTED MILK)
Yields 1 gallon

I debated about adding this recipe to the book because one has to be very comfortable with the idea of raw milk before the idea of fermenting will be appealing. However, because clabbered milk is a large part of how we use dairy, I decided that it deserves a place in this chapter.

INGREDIENTS

1 gallon raw milk

DIRECTIONS

Place clean, raw milk in a clean glass or stainless-steel container and cover to protect it against dirt. Place the milk in a warm spot in your kitchen. Traditionally, my grandma would set hers on the warming shelf of her wood-burning cookstove, and I set mine on top of my refrigerator in winter and on the counter in summer. It will take 2 to 6 days for the lactic acid bacteria to break down all the sugars and give you clabbered milk. You will know your milk has clabbered when it separates into a curd that rises to the top and a thin whey settles to the bottom.

Don't stir, shake, or disturb the milk while it is clabbering. When the milk has clabbered, remove ¼ cup of clabber and place into a clean jar. This is now your clabber starter, and you will add this starter to your raw milk the next time you want to make clabber.

Having a starter like this will speed up your clabbering process. Place your clabbered milk into the refrigerator, where it will keep for up to a month or more.

The pH of clabbered milk makes it perfect for replacing water or fresh milk in baking recipes, resulting in light and fluffy baked goods. I especially love to use clabber as my liquid when making sourdough bread. In my kitchen, clabber is also used in any recipe that calls for cultured dairy, such as buttermilk.

We use clabber to make cottage cheese, ricotta cheese, and a traditional Pennsylvania Dutch cheese called *Schmierkäse* (see recipe on page 191).

CULTURED DAIRY

Consuming cultured dairy has become a popular and trendy way to improve gut health, as it is scientifically proven that ingesting the probiotic family of beneficial bacteria aids in digestion. Store-bought cultured dairy like yogurt and kefir begins with pasteurized milk, and then the lab-grown bacteria is added to the pasteurized dairy and sold to you. But if you have access to raw milk, you have access to billions and billions of these beneficial bacteria for improving your family's health.

We also use clabber in place of kefir and make breakfast smoothies by adding some frozen fruit and maple syrup or honey.

Clabbered milk might be new to you, but it wasn't new to our refrigerator-less ancestors. Raw milk has naturally occurring lactic acid bacteria. You might better recognize these beneficial bacteria if I tell you that they are in the probiotic family of bacteria. As soon as the milk leaves the cow, the lactic acid bacteria goes to work breaking down the sugars in the milk. As the bacteria breaks down and feeds on the sugars, the milk changes from a sweet taste to more of a tart (sour) taste, the pH of the milk begins to fall, and the texture changes from a thin liquid to a thick, yogurt-like consistency. When this happens, you have clabbered milk (also known as naturally cultured, sour, or fermented milk). Since cold slows down the ability of the bacteria to work, we chill raw milk as soon as possible to preserve its sweet taste for fresh use and leave milk at room temperature or warmer if we want to clabber it.

SCHMIERKÄSE
Yields 2 cups

Schmierkäse (also called Amish Cup Cheese) is a cheese recipe that my ancestors brought with them to America around 1600 from their Swiss/German days. It's a soft, spreadable cheese that we ate as a snack or light meal, spread on homemade bread, or smeared on pretzels and crackers. Modern folks who have tasted it have likened its taste to that of French Brie, but since I haven't ever had Brie, it just tastes like Grandma's cheese to me.

INGREDIENTS

1 gallon clabbered milk

1½ tsp. baking soda

¼ cup melted butter

1 tsp. salt

¾ cup hot water

DIRECTIONS

Slowly heat your clabbered milk to 125°. My grandma's recipe didn't have a temperature recorded; it just read "Heat until clabber is very hot, not boiling but too hot to keep your finger in it." Give the heating clabber an occasional gentle stir to keep the curds from settling to the bottom and getting too hot. You'll see the curds separating from the whey more clearly as the temperature rises. Once the desired temp is reached, ladle or pour your curds and whey into a cheesecloth-lined colander. Tie up the corners of your cheesecloth and drain the curds for 2 to 3 hours.

My grandma would add a bit of fresh cream and a dash of salt to these dry curds and eat them with fresh fruit. This was my first introduction to cottage cheese, and I still prefer this version over any other form.

At this stage I also use the curds with a bit of fresh cream to replace ricotta cheese in recipes like lasagna and other Italian dishes.

Once your curds are dry (and if you haven't eaten them all as cottage cheese yet), put them into a heavy-bottom saucepan and add the baking soda. Stir in the baking soda well, making sure to break up any large curds. I use my hands here.

Rest the curds and baking soda for 30 minutes to an hour, then add your melted butter, salt, and hot water. Heat over low heat, stirring all the while, until curds are dissolved and cheese is smooth.

Add seasonings if you prefer; our favorite is to add some chopped, dried jalapeños. It tastes just like queso.

Schmierkäse stores well, covered, in the refrigerator for 2 to 3 weeks. Make sure you use plastic wrap or wax paper snug against the cheese to keep it from developing a dry crust.

Schmierkäse Tangy Grilled Cheese

If you want a unique grilled cheese sandwich that will soon become a family favorite, give this simple, surprising recipe a try.

Spread Schmierkäse generously on 1 piece of sourdough bread and then spread hot pepper jelly on another slice of sourdough, put together, and grill the sandwich in a cast-iron skillet with butter until it becomes a delectable, flavorful grilled cheese sandwich!

MOZZARELLA CHEESE
Yields 1½ pounds

This cheese gets all the credit for taking store-bought sandwich cheese off my grocery list. And although my family wouldn't normally choose mozzarella cheese for their sandwiches, they didn't complain when I started using it, and I felt a lot better about the nutrition in homemade mozzarella over the highly processed cheese slices we had been using. Since mozzarella doesn't need to be aged, it is a great beginner cheese to make once a week or more until you gain the confidence to try aged cheeses.

INGREDIENTS

2 gallons milk (any milk except ultra pasteurized; I skim most of the cream from my 2- to 3-day-old raw milk)

3 tsp. citric acid

1 tsp. liquid calf rennet (or the amount recommended on your bottle to coagulate 2 gallons milk)

⅔ cup salt

DIRECTIONS

Heat milk to 55°.
Dissolve citric acid in ½ cup cool water and add to milk; stir well.
Over low heat, slowly heat your milk to 88°.
Remove from heat.
Dissolve rennet in ½ cup cool water and stir into milk. Stir well using up and down motions to make sure rennet reaches the milk on the bottom too.
Cover your milk and let it sit for 10 to 15 minutes and then check for a clean break in the curd by sticking your finger at an angle into the curd and lifting it to break the curd over your finger. If the curd cracks apart with crisp edges, it's ready to cut. If the curd seems

to fall apart like a thin Jell-O, let sit for another 10 minutes and check again.

When you have crisp edges, cut your curds into 1- or 2-inch squares and then cover and rest for 5 to 10 minutes to allow curds to settle to the bottom.

Remove 2 to 3 cups of warm whey from the top of the curds and put into a clean bowl. To this whey, add your salt and stir to dissolve.

Start heating your curds over medium-low heat while stirring gently to break up the long cubes until all cubes are approximately the same size.

Gently stirring your curds will help them release their whey, and the heat will cause them to stick together. Keep gently stirring—I use my hands because I like to feel what is happening—until you can feel the curds start to clump together. As your whey heats, the curds will get soft and stretchy. This usually happens as the whey becomes too hot for my hands. Switch to wooden spoons or put on a pair of rubber kitchen gloves to continue.

Start stretching the cheese. If your whey is hot enough, you can just lift the cheese from the pot and let the weight of it do the stretching. Place the cheese back into the hot whey whenever it cools too much to keep stretching. The temperature your cheese starts to stretch will depend on the acid level and proteins of your milk; therefore, heat your whey until your cheese starts to stretch well and then stabilize your temperature. Stretching elongates the protein chain, giving the familiar stringy texture of mozzarella cheese. Stretch until each section has a shiny and smooth appearance.

Let the cheese rest on the bottom of the pot until it becomes soft and pliable and then shape it into a ball.

Remove your mozzarella ball from the hot whey. Place cheese into your bowl of salted whey and then refrigerate until chilled. Once chilled, remove from whey and wrap tightly in plastic wrap. Slice and use on sandwiches or grate for pizza. Fresh mozzarella keeps in the refrigerator for up to a week. After that, I grate it and store in the freezer for 6 or more months.

Variations:

String Cheese: When you are stretching your mozzarella, stretch into strings that are approximately as thick as your fingers. Use kitchen scissors to cut to desired length. Place in whey and chill and then wrap tightly for storing.

Basil Mozzarella Balls: Fill a pint jar with 1 cup of quality olive oil, 1 tablespoon of salt, and freshly chopped basil to taste. Stir to dissolve salt. When stretching your cheese, pull it into chunky ropes and use your scissors to cut into 1-inch squares. Place these squares into the pint jar. These will stay fresh at room temperature for 2 to 3 days. After that, store in the refrigerator for up to a week.

HOMESTEAD ICE CREAM
Yields 2 quarts

The creamy, cold deliciousness of this summertime treat is only made sweeter by the simplicity of the recipe.

DIRECTIONS

Mix all ingredients with an immersion blender or in a regular blender for 1 to 2 minutes. Let rest for 5 minutes and blend for another 2 to 3 minutes or until sugar is dissolved. Pour mixture into an ice cream machine and churn until desired consistency is reached.

Variations:

Coffee ice cream: Mix ¼ cup hot water and instant coffee granules until dissolved, add to ice cream mixture, and churn like usual.

Chocolate ice cream: Mix ½ cup hot water and cocoa until dissolved, add to ice cream mixture, and churn like usual.

Fruit ice cream: Add fresh fruit to ice cream 10 minutes before you stop the churn. Finish churning the ice cream.

Leftover homestead ice cream is the base of many delicious summer milkshakes for our family. We put the ice cream and any flavors we desire into the blender and whip it into a cool afternoon treat.

INGREDIENTS

4 cups (1 quart) heavy fresh cream

1 cup milk (whole or skim)

4 egg yolks

¾ cup granulated sugar

1 T. quality vanilla

¼ tsp. salt

Add-in Flavor Options:

1 T. instant coffee

¼ to ½ cup unsweetened cocoa

1 to 1½ cups finely chopped fresh fruit

CHAPTER SEVEN

THE ART OF THRIFTINESS

Gaining contentment through a budget-friendly lifestyle

The drawer was overflowing with squares of tinfoil, pieces of string, and plastic bags. If you dug deeper, you'd find more supplies: paper clips, twist ties, safety pins. Ziplock bags were never disposable at Grandma's house because she would wash them and I would pin them onto the line to let the wind fill them like a kite and dry them. Once dry, they were folded neatly and placed in the drawer to be used again. Tinfoil was always carefully cleaned, dried, and folded just as neatly, to be used again.

Grandma didn't throw things away. She didn't know a disposable world like we do now. The clothing and shoes they wore were worth mending. And Grandma always kept a couple boxes of dark-colored dye on hand to give old, stained clothing items a new chance at life.

I spent many nights at my grandma's house studying the handmade quilts covering my bed, trying to decide which pieces were original and which were patches covering holes. I wondered, *Why didn't she simply buy or make a new quilt?* As I used Grandma's laundry stick and plunged Grandpa's coat into the dark dye water, I no doubt had the questions, *Why didn't Grandma simply buy a new coat for Grandpa? Why didn't she buy a new box of ziplock bags or tinfoil?*

This important skill of thriftiness was fostered in my grandparents when the Great Depression affected their young adult lives.

Even the daily paper they received did not go to waste. It got cut up into squares that were then stacked in the outhouse to replace the modern convenience of toilet paper. Although Grandma did keep rolls of toilet paper to use when she invited company for Sunday dinner, the newspaper was for everyday use. Ironically, when the toilet paper shortage of 2020 happened and our children started getting worried about not having access to toilet paper, I felt a deep calm. I knew exactly what to do if we lost access to toilet paper, and according to Grandma's stories of her childhood, even corn cobs would work if we ran out of newspaper.

The conclusion that ten-year-old me came to was that Grandma and Grandpa were very poor indeed, and I took it upon myself to help them save every penny I possibly could. I became fully invested in helping Grandma be thrifty, whether when washing windows with newspapers, collecting grass clippings for her garden, or picking up corn from a newly harvested field for the horse. I never questioned the reason behind these chores once I knew that we were on a mission to not spend money unless we absolutely had to.

Of course, as I became older, I realized that my grandparents were, in fact, not poor at all. They had merely developed a worthwhile skill of living well within their means. This important skill of thriftiness was fostered in my grandparents when the Great Depression affected their young adult lives. The important lesson I want to remember from Grandma and Grandpa's thrifty lifestyle is that even when there was enough money to buy anything they needed, they didn't raise their standard of living. Instead, they kept their life simple and valued the little that they had.

HONORING THE COST AND VALUE OF ALL THINGS

It seems that the more readily we have access to something, the less we appreciate it!

Raising our own meat drove this lesson home for me because it takes two or more years to raise a beef cow. From that one cow, you get only two briskets. Those briskets became very valuable to me, and together with the family, we chose just the right occasion to smoke, serve, and enjoy them, fully understanding that it would be twelve to eighteen months before we would have access to more brisket.

The same with pork. Each hog yields about sixteen pounds of bacon. Our family can easily consume a whole pound of bacon in one breakfast. And I love to use bacon in my other meals too. This means for each hog we raise, we can have bacon for sixteen meals. If we eat one pound of bacon each week, we will be out of bacon long before we have another hog ready for harvest.

We can run out of chicken quickly too. There are only two breasts on each bird, so to feed my family a meal of chicken breast requires four whole birds.

Bacon, brisket, and chicken breast are therefore high-value meals and are saved for special occasions—not because we are poor, but because we are living within our means and being conscious consumers. We could afford to go to the grocery store and buy a pound or even two of bacon every week, and eventually it would lose its value to the family because we would've convinced the kids that there is an endless supply of bacon available for their dining pleasure and at no cost to them directly. Instead, because my entire family has invested time and effort caring for the piglets, fixing fences, and feeding the hogs, they are well aware of both the commitment of resources required, the cost to us, and the value of the limited amount of bacon. This is a life lesson in consumerism we want to give our children.

When we served brisket to the guests at our daughter's wedding and someone asked if we raised it ourselves, I had a pang of guilt when I realized that the amount of brisket that we fed the guests came from eight to ten cows. The amount of time and energy it takes to raise ten cows is not lost on me at all, and yet feeding our wedding guests was as simple as paying for the meat. Prior to raising our own meat, this conversation would not have given me a reason to pause.

My entire family has invested time and effort caring for the piglets.

MAXIMIZE YOUR RESOURCES

The value of things is directly related to how much time, effort, and resources we have invested in them. One of the biggest reasons folks don't take the next step on their journey of living more self-sustainably is that they think they lack resources. They believe they lack the obvious resources like land or finances. But when you really start thinking about what resources you do have, you will likely discover that you can take the next step after all.

Valuable resources:
Time
Skills
Finances
Space

If you have only one of these resources, you can move ahead! Here is how:

If you have time, even just an hour each week, you can use that time to gain skills. When you have skills, you can use them to gain finances, and when you have finances, you can use them to gain space.

Through this lens, time becomes one of the most valuable resources to have. No matter what your goals, time is what you can use to your benefit to move toward your goals.

The years when our finances were lacking were hard ones. There was definitely a moment when I was tempted to use my resource of time to add a second stream of income and alleviate the pressure of not having enough money. However, I didn't want to sacrifice time with my children in exchange for extra money. That cost was too high, in my opinion. So, I started to evaluate how I could use every little bit of time available to help us gain finances.

This looked like washing and drying my ziplock bags (just like Grandma did). It looked like replacing many grocery items with made-from-scratch versions. It looked like raising meat chickens and using that cheaper protein for many meals. It looked like mending our clothes. It looked like drying my laundry outside on a line (and indoors on drying racks in winter) instead of using my dryer. It often looked like doing without and waiting to find a used version of something we needed. It always looked like using my time and effort to save us money. And little by little it started adding up.

The more I saw the little five-dollar differences adding up, the more inspired I became. I realized that with little, intentional adjustments each day, I could control precisely how much of our money went to household expenses. It wasn't long before I had cut our household budget in half just by using my time and skills. This wiggle room in our budget, over time, gave us the resource of finances that we needed to make larger investments that would save us even more money in the long run—investments like a family milk cow and a breeding pair of hogs and a skid loader.

Although washing and reusing my ziplock bags and tinfoil helped, the largest impact on our budget was made by spending my time in the kitchen cooking from scratch instead of purchasing convenient and expensive versions of our diet at the grocery store. Homemade granola to replace boxed cereal saved us twenty-five dollars a week. Making bread, hamburger buns, and pasta saved us ten to twelve dollars each week. Popping corn and making homemade granola bars instead of relying on store-bought prepackaged snacks and chips saved us twenty to thirty dollars each week. A bonus to these adjustments was that, by controlling ingredients, we were cutting many harmful and unnecessary additives from my family's diet.

And yes, it takes more time and energy. Hanging laundry to dry is an investment of the time it takes to hang each load and then take it down. The folding and putting away of the laundry still takes the same amount of time. With a bit of extra time and effort invested on each laundry day, I saved us hundreds of dollars each year. This all added up to giving us room in our budget to not only purchase

With a bit of extra time and effort invested on each laundry day, I saved us hundreds of dollars each year.

a family milk cow but to put up a fence and purchase hay for her winter diet. And when the milk started flowing, we were able to cut back our grocery budget even further. Butter, cheese, yogurt, and all things dairy got crossed off our shopping list. This of course didn't happen in a month or even a year. It took time to form new habits and get accustomed to doing without. The harder we worked to save money, the more valuable it became to us. Every purchase made with hard-earned money was cherished and celebrated.

DISCERNING TO SAVE DOLLARS

Here are some questions to ask yourself before spending money:

Can I make this healthier and cheaper at home?

You of course can't learn to make everything all at once, but as your resource of time allows, choose one thing from your grocery list to learn to make at home, and then when you've mastered that one and fit it into your routine, choose another one. It can be as simple as making your own taco seasoning blend, ranch dressing, and mayo, or as complex as making your own pasta, yogurt, and laundry soap. This becomes empowering as you realize you are in complete control of how much money you leave at the grocery store each week.

It can be as simple as making your own taco seasoning blend, ranch dressing, and mayo, or as complex as making your own pasta, yogurt, and laundry soap.

Can I use time and effort to replace this convenience?

I find this question a good one to ask when needing to replace something. Dryer stopped working? Blender broke? Dishwasher quit? Does it really need to be replaced or can I save us money by using my time and effort and do without? When our dishwasher broke recently, instead of rushing out to replace it, we decided to take a year and have the entire family brush up on their dishwashing skills. It has now been well over a year, and no one has begged to purchase a dishwasher since the first few months. We have saved the money, and the bonus is that the elementary-age Zimmerman boys have developed some amazing dishwashing skills that will serve them well in their adult life. (And perhaps any future daughters-in-law will appreciate me!)

I remember begging my own mother to buy a dishwasher for our family. She would look at her six daughters and say, "Why should we spend the money on buying a dishwasher when I have six dishwashers?" We never did get a dishwasher in that old farmhouse. My five sisters and I shared the chore of washing dishes for our family of eleven, and while doing what seemed like an endless number of dishes, we made some of my fondest childhood memories in our kitchen and even at that kitchen sink.

Only once did I ever complain to my grandma about having to wash dishes. She smiled and said, "Well, you only need to wash dishes until you learn to like it and then you may quit." When, after washing a few more pieces, I happily announced to Grandma that I had now learned to love washing dishes, she cheerfully replied, "That's great news, and if you have truly learned to love it, then you will surely finish the dishes with a cheerful attitude."

Is this a want or a need?

Another reason to pause before making a purchase is to evaluate if the purchase is a want or a need. While a new dryer or dishwasher might seem like a need and a milk cow might fall into your want category, I would argue that it's the other way around. Saving for a milk cow is a more immediate need for your family, because with a little time, the milk cow will help you begin to save money on your grocery bill, and in the end, you'll have saved enough to purchase the item that was a "want" like a dishwasher (if you still want it).

The question I ask myself when I'm not sure I can do without a convenience is, "How did Grandma manage without a blender, a dryer, or a kitchen mixer?" Most of the time the answer is simply that she used a little more time and effort than I've become accustomed to using. A little more effort is required to whip the eggs, butter, and sugar by hand than with the mixer. It takes a little more effort to roll the pasta dough by hand than it does to use the pasta machine.

Often I find myself choosing to do things with my hands, the simple and uncomplicated way that Grandma did it, because once I become used to it, it actually takes less time and effort. I eventually found that rolling and cutting my pasta by hand and having one rolling pin to wash took much less time and effort than messing with the machine setup, and then washing, drying, and storing it. Now I typically choose to use a sharp knife over setting up my blender and then having to wash and put it away. The value of a single quality knife is more to me than a $300 blender, because with that knife, I could replace numerous modern kitchen appliances if I needed to.

Every convenience gained is a skill lost.

Being able to separate wants from needs is a skill that develops over time and with practice. The willingness to spend time and effort to make up for lack of convenience becomes easier with practice. As you learn to cook from scratch you will become accustomed to the extra time (and dishes) that the kitchen requires, and eventually you will notice all the little changes you've been making along the way have added up to be a big lifestyle change!

While the modern world tempts us with the latest contraptions and conveniences, wisdom comes in knowing the value of your time and the benefits of working with your hands, then deciding for yourself if the convenience is worth the price and the time you would save. Think of it this way: Every convenience gained is a skill lost.

Invest your time in skills and encourage your family to do the same. There will be many rewards reaped because of that shift. Some will be monetary benefits, but there will also be rewards of character, fortitude, discernment, and the freedom to do what suits your family, your situation, and your life.

Every convenience gained is a skill lost.

THRIFTING TIPS

Thrifting provides us with the thrill of the hunt. You never know what you're going to find, and not every trip to a thrift store or consignment shop will be successful. But those trips when you spy an item that makes your heart skip a beat will keep you coming back for more. It could be a rare edition of a favorite book, an antique mirror for that empty wall, or a wool coat with a hood that promises to make winter chores more comfortable.

First, find a local, clean thrift or consignment shop and be a frequent shopper but not a frequent buyer. Shopping frequently means that you won't need to spend a lot of time because you will be able to spot new items immediately, in this way saving you the time and effort of browsing the whole store.

Then learn to shop from the racks and shelves that have just been pushed out onto the floor, as these contain the newest items.

Most importantly, learn to be comfortable walking out the door without a purchase. You are not shopping for clutter but for quality items that add value to your home and homestead.

What I Look For at the Thrift Store

- Wool clothing or blankets of any kind (durable, warm, and worth mending or repurposing)
- Wool rugs
- Sheep skins
- Quality winter boots (or any footwear) in the sizes the family is growing into
- Heavy-bottom pots with lids (especially large sizes for preserving large amounts of garden veggies)
- Stainless steel dishes and bowls
- Cast iron of any kind
- Glass dishes with lids
- Cutting boards
- Quality knives
- Kitchen gadgets like shredders, graters, and grinders that are not electric
- Quality furniture

SCHOOL OF THRIFTING SKILLS

Consider yourself a student in the school of thrifting skills. There is always more to learn and discover. Make saving an extra enjoyable pursuit by connecting with others in your community or online who are further ahead in the skill mastery or who want to learn as much as you do. Here are just a few of the areas to explore as you work to expand your knowledge and skills over time. Remember, every little step toward being a saver and frugal shopper will serve you and your family.

Buying quality used items: Quality used items often have more life left in them than new items of the same price.

Dying fabrics: Discover which fabrics can be dyed and then how to do it.

Mending: Learn which items are worth mending and how to do it.

Cooking from scratch: Choose one or two items from your grocery list at a time and learn to prepare them in a way that your family loves.

Gardening: Determine which crops grow easily in your area and learn to grow those.

Preserving: Research how to preserve what you grow, or buy fruits and veggies that are on sale and preserve those.

Freezing: Purchase a deep freezer and buy "on sale" items and freeze them for later use.

Drying Laundry: Dry your laundry outdoors instead of in the dryer.

Doing Dishes: Wash dishes by hand instead of using the dishwasher.

HOMEMADE LAUNDRY DETERGENT

Makes enough for 128 loads

DIRECTIONS

Grate the entire bar of Fels-Naptha and add to 4 cups hot water in a heavy-bottom pot. Heat over medium-high heat, stirring continuously until the soap is dissolved. Don't allow it to boil over; this creates a huge mess.

Once soap is dissolved, remove from heat, add the washing soda and Borax, and continue to stir until the powders are dissolved.

Add 4 cups warm water and stir until incorporated. Cool and store. This is your concentrate. Use approximately 1 tablespoon per load of laundry.

Alternately, dilute the concentrate with more water to help it dispense from a liquid detergent dispenser, and use ⅓ cup detergent per load.

This will do approximately 128 loads of laundry.

INGREDIENTS

1 (5 oz.) bar Fels-Naptha (found at most grocery stores)

8 cups water, divided

1 cup Borax

1 cup washing soda

VINEGAR CLEANING SOLUTION
Makes 1 quart

DIRECTIONS

Put peels into a glass quart jar, then fill to the top with vinegar until peels are all covered. Store for 3 to 4 weeks, strain, and you have a concentrated cleaner that is tough on dirt, grease, and grime.

Add ¼ cup to a gallon of water for general cleaning.

Mix 1 part solution to 1 part water in a spray bottle for heavier spot cleaning.

Using white vinegar without the citrus peel infusion works too, but the smell is not as pleasant.

INGREDIENTS

Peels of 2 to 3 oranges, lemons, or grapefruits

Distilled white vinegar

TALLOW LOTION
Makes 1 pint

DIRECTIONS

Melt tallow and liquid oil together. I like to use jojoba oil or grapeseed oil, but any light liquid oil will work. Once melted, chill in the refrigerator until mixture reaches a soft Jell-O consistency. Add any optional ingredients. With an immersion blender or whisk, blend until lotion is light and creamy. Store at room temperature for 3 to 4 months and use for all your family's moisturizing needs.

INGREDIENTS

1 cup tallow (beef fat)

1 cup liquid oil

Optional:

1 T. liquid vitamin E oil

Essential oils

WHERE YOUR TREASURE LIES
A few last and lasting words

I'm up to my elbows in dishwater, scrubbing away at a pan that was left to soak by one of the children. Family dinner is over, and the beautiful weather has coaxed everyone to the backyard. In the moments of peace that I'm afforded by being the one who will tidy the kitchen, I mentally check off the things that need to be done so I can, as Grandma used to say, "put the kitchen to bed": Scrub the pots and pans that were left for ruin, clean the stovetop, wipe the countertop and refrigerator front, clean out the drain traps. This is how Grandma and Mom taught me to leave the kitchen each evening—sparkling and ready for a new day. That kind of ritual chore becomes tradition.

And yet, through the open window, I hear the family calling for me. They want me to join the backyard ball game they have set up, the game that I know from experience will endanger my zinnias, sweet peas, and anything else growing on the north side of the garden.

Leaving the dishes behind, I wipe my hands on my apron and exchange it for a softball glove on my hand. With a hasty last glance at a kitchen that would make my grandma grimace and scold me, I use a familiar Bible passage to remind myself once again that only souls are eternal, and a sparkling kitchen has no eternal value.

I use a familiar Bible verse to remind myself once again that only souls are eternal.

It's the passage that I use daily to help balance the work of the homestead and family and keep my priorities organized.

This passage helps me value a ball game with the family over the beautiful zinnias in my garden.

This passage reminds me how the people God has put into my life are more important than keeping our house tidy or filling our larder and freezers with homegrown fruits, veggies, and meats.

This passage reminds me that if we reach every goal but miss the opportunities to draw the souls of our family and loved ones toward the light of the world, then it will all have been for naught.

> *Lay not up for yourselves treasures upon earth, where moth and rust doth corrupt, and where thieves break through and steal: But lay up for yourselves treasures in heaven, where neither moth nor rust doth corrupt, and where thieves do not break through nor steal: For where your treasure is, there will your heart be also.*
> MATTHEW 6:19-21 KJV

The family counted me in, and the game started. Now I am up to bat. I look out at my kids and my husband. Beyond them I see the fields, fences, and barn. This is my heart. I smile . . . there is so much joy here, and still, I am certain there are even sweeter eternal treasures beyond this moment, beyond this homestead.

RECIPE INDEX

Canning
    Apple or Pear Butter 131
    Apple Pie Filling 128
    Beets, Pickled 124
    Blueberry Pie Filling 128
    Chili Base 118
    No-Pectin Jams 129
    Pasta Sauce 117
    Pickles, Hamburger Dill 120
    Pickles, Sweet Dill 123
    Pie Filling 128
    Pineapple Zucchini 127
    Potatoes, Dry Canned 125
    RuthAnn's Canned Chicken and Broth 160
    Salsa 119
Caramel Popcorn 62
Chicken
    Chicken Noodle Soup 161
    Roasted Whole Chicken 154
    Thanksgiving Amish Roast 156
Chili 118
Cream Soup 63
Dairy
    Basil Mozzarella Balls 194
    Browned Butter 186
    Butter 185
    Chocolate Ice Cream 195
    Chocolate Milk 188
    Clabber (Fermented Milk) 189
    Coffee Ice Cream 195
    Fruit Ice Cream 195
    Homestead Ice Cream 195
    Mozzarella Cheese 192
    Schmierkäse 191
    Schmierkäse Tangy Grilled Cheese 192
    String Cheese 194
Egg Noodles (Homemade Pasta) 153
Green Bean Casserole 63
Granola Bars 62
Gravy 161
Ham and Bean Soup 155
Mom's Pumpkin Pie 159
Red Beet Eggs (Pickled Eggs) 157
White Bread 61

Household and Self-Care
    Homemade Laundry Detergent 214
    Mildew Prevention and Treatment for Plants 87
    Natural Bug Repellent for Plants 90
    Tallow Lotion 215
    Vinegar Cleaning Solution 215

ACKNOWLEDGMENTS

First, I want to acknowledge the people who believed I could author a book: my husband, Elvin, and Ruth, my editor. Without your belief in me I would still believe that social media captions are the extent of my writing skill set.

My four older children, Kristina, Staci, Mitchell, and Hadassah, for teaching me about parenting the heart, for reading raw materials that I shoved under your noses, and for encouraging me by telling me, "That's good, Mom!"

My three little boys, Maxwell, Kendrick, and Harrison, for teaching me that even though I'll never be able to harness and direct your collective energy, I can have profound influence over your hearts. Thanks for being proud of me even when you could not understand a word I wrote.

And finally, I want to acknowledge my church family at Gospel Lighthouse Church. Without the prayer warriors there, this book would still be only a dream.

ABOUT THE AUTHOR

RuthAnn and her family live in Northeast Iowa. She and her husband, Elvin, have been married for twenty-five years. They have seven children, two sons-in-law, and one grandson. RuthAnn and her husband have been homesteading on their 21-acre homestead since 2001. They seek to preserve the self-sufficient lifestyle of their Old Order Mennonite heritage for the next generation by involving their children in every aspect of the homestead, from raising and harvesting the meat they consume, gardening and preserving to fill the family's larder, and processing the dairy from the family milk cow, to the many other skills that develop the character, integrity, and relationships of a family who desires to bring glory and honor to their heavenly Father.